Reflections from the Parlor

A Pilgrim's Spiritual Journey

Jean B. Burden

TEL Publishing
Huntersville, NC

For further information please contact
Jean B. Burden at lilymom7@gmail.com

Copyright © 2015 by Jean B. Burden
Cover Design: Stephen Lursen Art
Cover Photo: Dan Burden
Published by: TEL Publishing

ISBN: 978-0-9910989-4-1

Scripture taken from the New International Version® unless otherwise noted.

Scripture taken from the Holy Bible, New International Version®, NIV®, Copyright © 1973, 1978, 1984, 2011 by Biblica, Inc., ™. Used by permission of Zondervan. All rights reserved worldwide. www.zondervan.com The "NIV" and "The New International Version" are Trademarks registered in the United States Patent and Trademark Office by Biblica, Inc., ™

Scripture quotations from the New King James Version®. Copyright © 1982 by Thomas Nelson, Inc. Used by permission. All rights reserved.

Scripture quotations from THE MESSAGE. © by Eugene H. Peterson 1993, 1994, 1995, 1996, 2000, 2001, 2002. Used by permission of Tyndale House Publishers, Inc.

Library of Congress Cataloging-in-Publication Data
Burden, Jean B., 1958 -

reflections from the parlor : a pilgrim's spiritual journey

Library of Congress Control Number: 2014953545

Dedication

I would like to dedicate this book to God, the provider of and the inspiration behind everything of value in my life. Thank You for ordering my steps and allowing a humble servant to love and encourage people in Your Name.

God can do anything, you know---far more than you could ever imagine or guess or request in your wildest dreams! He does it not by pushing us around but by working within us, his Spirit deeply and gently within us.
Glory to God in the church!
Glory to God in the Messiah, in Jesus!
Glory down all the generations!
Glory through all the millennia! Oh, yes!
(Ephesians 3:20-21, The Message)

Acknowledgments

With special thanks:

To my publisher and friend, Terry Lursen, for guiding and making the painful process of editing not so painful

To my Facebook readers, who believed in me and encouraged me to write a book

To Jentzen Franklin, who doesn't know me, but whose book about fasting and praying sent me to the parlor for the first time

To my husband Dan, who created "the parlor," giving me a beautiful space to retreat and find God

To my children, grandchildren, husband, friends, students and pets, who have been the stories behind the words

Introduction

Let me open with a warning: I am not a trained Bible scholar or an expert on all matters spiritual. What I am is a daughter of God, wholly and completely dedicated to write what He nudges me to write, sing what He nudges me to sing, say what He nudges me to say, and do everything He tells me to do. *Everything...* Even write a book!

Quite a number of years ago, God used someone else's book to impress upon me that I need more than just church and religion; I needed an ongoing, deep relationship with my Father and Savior. From that day until this one, I have continued to grow that relationship and deepen my knowledge of God through study and prayer.

At some time during this growth, God encouraged me to write, always giving me the topic through simple things I saw and experienced around me while walking out this journey called life. I never once imagined writing a book. I simply posted my writings on Facebook, and God used other Christian friends to say, "You really need to publish a book." And so here we are. These writings span the last five or six years, and every single topic came from the Holy Spirit speaking into my spirit. I simply am not smart enough to do this on my own, but God has guided every step!

Just a few years ago, I found myself in a room of my house that I call "the parlor." No TV, no internet, no distractions, just peacefulness and a space to connect with God. And in January of 2011, as I fasted and prayed, seeking God's will for that year, some things happened in my life that would have devastated me without God's strength and power. There were days in the parlor that I simply cried, calling out God's name, and yes, there were days that I lay prostrate before Him, saying, "I can't do this!" But He quietly and lovingly said, "Yes, you can." He carried me through those difficult days, bringing me out stronger and more grateful for His hand than ever before. I still pray and rest in that parlor, knowing that I always find God's guidance as I enter that space. He has been good to me, and I want to share what I have learned about Him with you.

As you read the pages of this book, I encourage you to take them slowly, maybe reading one a day or every other day, but probably reading just one a week. There are 40 devotionals here, simply because that is the number God gave me to share. 40 days in the desert, 40 years in the wilderness, 40 days and nights of rain as Noah trusted God. The number just seemed right and perfect, and so there are 40. Take them slowly, and use the scriptures built into the writing or given at the end of each piece as a place of study and meditation. Let those words --- God's words --- speak into your spirit, asking the Holy Spirit to guide you into all truth as you ponder them and how they apply to your life.

I pray that you will be blessed by spending time with me on this journey from my parlor. I also pray that in spending time in meditation, study, and prayer, you will see how God can use you and your destiny to glorify Him and further His kingdom. My journey with Him has been full of mountain tops and valleys, as it will continue to be, but every single experience has been covered by God. Trust Him, as I do, to be your everything.

Be blessed,

Jean Burden

September, 2014

Contents

I Don't Know Much

There was a memorable, award winning duet recorded by Aaron Neville and Linda Ronstadt in 1989 (boy, that dates me!), and in romantic fashion, they sang that sometimes its simply enough to know that we love someone. It was one of those songs that captured my attention from the first time I heard it, and I can even remember where I was when it first came on the radio: the parking lot of Myrtle Square Mall in Myrtle Beach, SC, which also dates me since that mall doesn't exist anymore! I loved it because it was romantic and because I love melodic duets, but recently God used those words to speak to me in another way.

I have been in a very hard season lately . . . a stagnant season, a dry season . . . and through it all, I have learned some urgent lessons, but the most important one God has shown me is this: life must be about *knowing* Him, about *seeking* His face, about just *loving* Him first and foremost.

And in the words of the song, this is enough for me to know.

Right now, I don't know exactly what my future holds, but I know that I am passionately, tenaciously and gloriously in love with God. I am hungry once again to know His word because it helps me to know *Him*. I am content to linger in His presence and know He is there. I have accepted that He is not going to show me everything right now, but Christ, the light of the world, is going to give me enough light for where I am today, enough light to see where I'm standing right now and just a tiny bit ahead.

Enough light to see into a God-given dream.

The Bible tells us that when we delight in Him, He will give us the desires of our heart, and I desire to know Him. I also desire to serve Him through music and testimony, and I know that He will honor that in His time and in His way, and it will be exceedingly and abundantly more than I can ask or think. I am dreaming big, but His dreams are bigger, and so it's enough to know Him...to call him Father and Friend. I desire to share my thoughts, concerns, and dreams, to converse with Him . . . the maker of the universe and the waterer of my dry season. He will do that for all of us, salvaging our arid deserts in the dry season until the rains come, and they *do* come.

So for now, I don't know much, but I know I love You, Lord, and that is definitely all I need to know.

And it's all you need to know as well. Love Him, and know that He loves you, too . . . unconditionally and completely . . . just as you are.

"Now to Him who is able to do above and beyond all that we ask or think according to the power that works in us --- to Him be glory in the church and in Christ Jesus to all generations, forever and ever." (Ephesians 3: 20-21)

Friends in Very High Places

Garth Brooks made a lot of money singing about friends in low places. I'm glad that he found success with that song, but it's been on my mind lately that I'm glad those are *his* words, *not mine*. I'm glad that is *his* story, *not mine*. It's a worldly message but it's not God's message. As a Christian, I want to sing and shout with thanksgiving and praise that I've got friends in high places. Think about it.

In the words of the insurance commercial, "Life comes at you fast," and it's where we've all lived at one time or another, some of us in recent days. Satan attacks, and worldly life as we know it starts to crumble. We make poor choices, and consequences are inevitable. We get dealt an unfair hand . . . a hand called cancer or infidelity or the untimely death of a child. Does life sometimes seem totally unfair? You better believe it! But here's the good news: we've got friends in high places, and lots of them.

We've got angels. God promises us that He sends angels to watch over us.

We've got Christian brothers and sisters. God always provides those intercessors who walk this earthly journey but live a life of prayer unceasing – a pretty "high place" to dwell. When they pray intercessory prayers on our behalf, they are lifting us into God's presence and into His mighty hands.

And best of all, we've got God. To say He's in "high places" is an understatement. Scripture says, "How lovely is Your dwelling place," and "Better is one day in Your courts than a thousand elsewhere." He lives on high in that lovely dwelling place, planning for us, listening to us, blessing us, and desiring to be in relationship with us. From heaven, He looks down on us with love, guiding our steps toward His perfect will. And when we're under attack, He says we need to cast our cares on Him because He cares for us. He hurts when we hurt, but our Father God on high wants us to depend on Him at all times... and especially in the dark times . . . He wants us to fall on our knees in prayer and praise. He wants us to trust that He can, and does, take every situation in our lives, turning it and using it for good.

Sound impossible? Good. That's when God's glory is at its best . . . when only *He* can fix things and we let Him. We get helped and He gets the glory.

Friends in high places? I've got plenty, and I am grateful. Why don't you join me today in thanking God for being the ultimate friend in the ultimate "high place."

Psalm 84: 1-2, "How lovely is Your dwelling place, Lord of Hosts. I long and yearn for the courts of the Lord; my heart and flesh cry out for the living God."

Psalm 84:10a, "Better a day in Your courts than a thousand anywhere else."

Psalm 91:9-11, "Because you have made the Lord --- my refuge, the Most High --- your dwelling place, no harm will come to you; no plague will come near your tent. For He will give His angels orders concerning you, to protect you in all your ways."

Luke 4:10, "For it is written: 'He will command His angels concerning you to guard you carefully.'

Made in the U.S.A.

Made in the USA. It's become a big issue in recent years, and stores like Wal-Mart make it a point to advertise in a huge way when items are made right here at home. I assume this has happened for two reasons: 1)Too much production work has been sent overseas, and in our failing economy, it's important to celebrate and promote American workers and their craft. 2) Stores are trying to re-create a sense of pride in our own country. Just look at Chevrolet's commercial that features the song "Strong." Everything in it celebrates the everyday life of Americans, and this is great. But how many times lately have you looked at the world around you and thought, "Made by God." I'm afraid we too often miss His creations because we are too busy and they aren't wearing a big tag like our clothing. Let's slow down and reconsider.

Last night I was driving home from church when I looked to my left and saw the most beautiful sight: a sliver of a crescent moon and one single star. It was breathtaking. I quickly called my granddaughter Lily because she loves the moon. I wanted to make sure she had a chance to see it and be amazed; she did, and she was. My daughter called me later, sharing that she took Lily outside, and the first thing out of her mouth was "Wow." Now, she is just over two years old, and she gets it: God's creations are worth a "wow" every time we stop to notice. Whitney allowed Lily to call me later, and in her sweet, tiny voice, she said, "A-ma, I saw the moon and the star," (Which sounded like "da moon and da star ☺). I shared with her that God made them both, just like he made her, and she is fearfully and wonderfully made. What an awesome concept for us to remember every day and share with others! God made it all, and we should stand in awe of the things that wear the tag, "Made by God."

In Psalm 19, we find these words: (from *The Message*)

[1-2] "God's glory is on tour in the skies,
     God-craft on exhibit across the horizon.
[3-4] Their words aren't heard,
     their voices aren't recorded,
But their silence fills the earth:
     unspoken truth is spoken everywhere.

[4-5] God makes a huge dome
     for the sun—a superdome!
The morning sun's a new husband
     leaping from his honeymoon bed,
The daybreaking sun an athlete
     racing to the tape.

[6] That's how God's Word vaults across the skies
     from sunrise to sunset,
Melting ice, scorching deserts,
     warming hearts to faith."

Wow. God made all of this to warm our hearts and show us His glory. We have the humbling privilege each day and each night to gaze in all directions and see His creations. From the crescent moon, suspended in space to the wildflowers in a field...from the colorful splendor of a rainbow to the total darkness of a stormy night with no stars in sight. From the trustworthy sunrise to the dependability of dusk. From the ocean's panorama to the mountain's majesty. Made by God. And yet we are so quick to forget . . . to take it for granted . . . to run through our days worrying about the events to come and not stopping to appreciate the canvas unfolding before our eyes. It's time to slow down.

In over fifty years of singing "church" music, one of my favorite anthems is still an old one – "The Majesty and Glory of Your Name." The music is incredible, making me want to close my eyes and drink it in, but the words are what get me every time: they remind to look into the heavens and see God's awesome handiwork.

And then it says that little children should praise him with perfect hearts, and so should we.

And so should we. Even in her young mind, Lily understands the beauty of God's creations. My favorite picture of her and her sister, Harper, is the two of them standing at an open window of their home. It was a stormy afternoon, and they wanted to "touch" the storm. Their tiny hands are outstretched in hopes of feeling the rain on their fingers. God made that storm, and we should stretch our fingers out to Him, too, praising Him in the thunderstorms of His creation. I personally think they are some of His most amazing work, and in a storm, you will always find me on the porch, rocking and cherishing every minute of the thunder and rain. Praising Him in a storm . . . there's another message for another day!

I want to close by telling you about an old friend. She was one of my roommates in college, and the first thing I learned about her was that labels mattered. She showed us every designer label in her clothes and bragged about how she would marry a man who could afford to buy her those expensive tags. She did marry that man, and it didn't work. She found out that the labels and money can't buy happiness, and sadly, she and her husband divorced, but at least she learned a valuable lesson: the only labels that will secure our joy are the ones that say, "Made by God." Marriages made by God, children who are fearfully and wonderfully made by God, and the stunning beauty of nature...made by God. Take time today to thank Him for His magnificent creations; don't let their beauty pass you by. It's worth taking time to read these tags and be blessed.

Lessons from Buck

As classic literature goes, *The Call of the Wild* by Jack London is a favorite of mine, and I absolutely love Buck, the central character. I connect with him for a number of reasons, not the least of which is his tenacious spirit of survival. We could all learn a lot of truth from Buck, the "dominant primordial beast."

Buck, like many of us, starts life with ease and simplicity, but after being sold into slavery, everything easy disappears and he must learn a new set of rules for living. Have you felt that way lately? Been in a marriage that started out on an idyllic path but took a terrible, torturous turn? Been in a job that seemed perfect but left you with a jaded perspective and little joy? Buck found himself in that situation, but rather than give in, he got smart. He became alert to danger and cognizant of when he needed to back out of a no-win situation, and we can become that smart, too. Buck's smarts came from a desire to survive and from his own natural instincts; our "smarts" need to come from God's Word. We have to dig deeply into scripture to know how to keep our joy when we're down, how to be still and wait on God for relief, and how to persevere by leaning on God's perfect strength rather than our own fallible power.

I also love Buck because he never saw himself, even in the worst situation, as an underdog, and neither should we. Though our circumstances may look one way . . . defeated . . . scripture promises that we are more than conquerors through Christ who strengthens us. We must see ourselves as God sees us: tenacious warriors whose strength is renewed when we wait upon God and wear His full armor into battle. But, there's more, and this is what I love about Buck so much.

Buck ended up being rescued by a new master, John Thornton, who treats him with loving kindness and Buck's response to that is to love that man with unbridled passion. He would . . . and does . . . do anything to please Thornton . . . "for the love of a man." Isn't that how we should be about God? Shouldn't we be so grateful that He saved us through grace that we would do absolutely anything to please Him? Buck was tempted by the "call of the wild," but he stayed in a relationship with his master out of deep, passionate love and just like Buck, I want to be so in love with God, my Master and Savior, that though I am tempted by Satan to be drawn away into sin, God remains my magnificent obsession... the desire of my heart, the relationship that drives and guides all else in my life.

And this is where the analogy ends. In the novel, John Thornton is killed by the Yeehats. Buck attacks his killers, and then, with no human ties left on earth, he answers the call of the wild. But we don't face this because our God is an everlasting God . . . a *living* Redeemer . . . a Creator who is still on the job every day, transforming you and me into new creations in Christ. The only "call of the wild" we must answer is the call of God's prevenient grace -- the call to love God wildly and with abandon -- and I am answering that call every day. I pray, sisters and brothers; that you will run with me, straight into the arms of Jesus. He is the one who forgives our sins and loves us like no other. Answering God's call on your life will be answering your personal call of the wild because life with Christ is a wild and wonderful ride of loving, believing, serving, and worshiping the one true God. What a ride!

Romans 12: 1-2, "Therefore, brothers, by the mercies of God, I urge you to present your bodies as a living sacrifice, holy and pleasing to God; this is your spiritual worship. Do not be conformed to this age, but be transformed by the renewing of your mind, so that you may discern what is the good, pleasing and perfect will of God."

Brokenness

In our culture, broken things are worthless: the stuff of dumpsters, and cheap yard sales and bottom drawers full of things we never intend to fix or use but can't quite throw away. Life cements this concept in our minds from an early age. Our mothers, not mine ...but some, rant and rave when we break a precious dish that once belonged to a dead aunt. Our fathers, not mine, either, mutter and curse silently when we break a favorite bass fishing rod. Our friends never speak to us again when we break a trust. You know this lesson well and yet, there is a joy to brokenness when seen with new eyes . . . God's eyes . . . eyes of a fallible, cracked human being who doesn't want to believe she's worthless. God's truth about our brokenness changes the entire landscape.

Before learning this from God, I got a fresh perspective from my husband who never sees things as broken junk but as possibilities for new creations. It makes me laugh to think of just last week – he went to the trash dump – the "recycling" center – and came back with these "really cool wooden things." "One man's trash is another man's treasure" is his philosophy and it has served him well. It serves God well, too.

God uses the brokenness in our lives to teach us, mature us, prepare us for a new thing He wants to do through us. In scripture we know that before Jesus fed the multitudes. He broke the bread and blessed it. That's how God works, breaking us of ego, and willfulness and any other "fleshly" thing before He can bless us and give us to the multitudes --- *His* multitudes. But why does He need to do it this way? Why can't it just be easy?

If it were easy, we would never give Him the credit.

We would be sure, in our puffed-up human way, that we know everything and can accomplish it on our own terms, and it's simply a lie. We need Him . . . and He needs us to need Him. So in recent years, I've come to embrace the messes I've made and the tests I've endured, because God has turned, in the words of Joel Osteen, my "mess into a message," and in Joyce Meyer's words, my "test into a testimony."

Blessed to be broken . . . the world won't get it, but I do.

2 Corinthians 12: 9-10, "And He said to me, 'My grace is sufficient for you, for My strength is made perfect in weakness.' Therefore most gladly I will rather boast in my infirmities, that the power of Christ may rest upon me. Therefore I take pleasure in infirmities, in reproaches, in needs, in persecutions, in distresses for Christ's sake. For when I am weak, then I am strong." (NKJV)

Belle's Love and the Porch

Belle – my loving yellow lab, named after my grandmother, Belle Mouzon – is a joy in my life. Belle is a special personality and I love her quirkiness. She is just under two years old and she loves my cats. She "fleas" Frankenstein and Figaro every day and carries them around the yard in her mouth. She wants very much to be their mother and doesn't care that she is not a cat; she only knows that she loves them and wants to be their mother. But this is not Belle's only special quality. Belle is a stereotypical lab, loving her owners with passion and her unbridled love for us reminds me of how I ought to behave when it comes to God.

Yesterday morning, I headed to my porch . . .my hiding place. I hide from distractions and people and I seek God. It is a place of rest for my soul, a place to savor God's Presence. But lately, Belle has wanted to come into the porch with me as I study and pray. Usually this is no big deal; she greets me, climbs in my lap as she only does this with me since Dan makes her behave, licks me in the face a few times and then settles onto the floor to nap near my feet. But not yesterday, yesterday was different, or should I say, Belle was different. She put her paws on my lap, licked my face with passion and refused to get down. No matter how many times I pushed her paws away, she came right back, greeting me with her sloppy kisses and her love. I couldn't stop her, so I decided to give up on reading and enjoy the moment. As she continued with her unassuming display of affection, I had a quiet, a-ha moment, 'God wants us to love Him and approach Him in just this way...every morning, every day, all day'.

The Bible tells us to seek God and in the words of one of my favorite songs, make Him our "magnificent obsession." He wants us to be deeply in love with Him and just like Belle, I want to love Him so much that I crawl into His lap showering Him with my adoration, awe, and passion for Him as my Father, my Comforter, my Friend, my Redeemer and my Savior. He wants us to seek Him in the morning, in the quiet place and spend time with Him there making Him the sole focus of our attention and our desires. He wants us to love Him unashamedly and be consumed with the utter joy of resting in His Presence.

As I finish writing this morning, I'm heading out to see Belle and visit with my God. I will enjoy loving Belle and allowing her to shower me with affection; I will do the same with my Father and can you imagine anything better? We have the awesome privilege of being in relationship with the Creator of the universe, the Savior of the world and the Healer of our land. Don't miss the opportunity today to love Him with passion and receive His love because in His Presence, there is fullness of joy.

Psalm 16: 11, "You reveal the path of life to me; in Your presence is abundant joy; in Your right hand are eternal pleasures."

Multitasker? Superwoman? Or Just Plain Just Tired...

Do you ever get tired of multitasking? I do and yet I'm totally addicted. I wake up and within minutes, the coffee is brewing while I say my first good morning to God all the while being dragged around by a 12-pound dog on a mission to smell the entire yard while doing her morning "business." On Saturdays during the school year . . . yes, a teacher . . . I feel the need to do as many things at once as possible: start the washer and while it's running, make the bed and call my Dad. Then it's on to other things . . . never doing just one thing at a time.

And the bottom line...I'm tired...*really* tired

So during this summer of 2010, I have practiced the art of slowing down and doing one thing at a time. But the reason I've been able to do this is that I have the ultimate multitasker taking care of me: God. I'm sure that we humans think we have a lock on being busy and keeping a myriad of balls in the air like a master juggler, but we are sorely mistaken. God figured that out years ago and this is why He is all we need.

Need a Father? He is there. "For the Father Himself loves me because I have loved Him and believed that He came out from the Father." (John 16:27)

Need a Healer? He's on that, too, "He heals my broken heart and binds up my wounds." (Ps. 147: 3)

Need a Comforter? Yeah, He's got it covered. "I call out to High God, the God who holds me together. He sends orders from heaven and saves me. God delivers generous love; He makes good on His

word." (Psalm 57:2-3)

Need a Forgiver? He's been doing that for . . . well, for *forever*. "If we confess our sins, He is faithful and just to forgive us our sins and to cleanse us from all unrighteousness." (1 John 1:9)

And the most amazing thing is that He does all of these and more at the same moment, every moment, every day, for every person who calls on His name.

So, if I have learned something this summer, it's this: I can never out-multitask God and I don't want to even try. I want to sit in His presence, spend time talking with and listening to the Creator of the Universe and cast my cares on Him. After all, He can handle them all at once . . . and He doesn't get ulcers! Cool, huh? Way cool.

"The Lord is my shepherd; there is nothing I lack. He lets me lie down in green pastures; He leads me beside quiet waters. He renews my life; He leads me along the right paths for His name's sake. Even when I go through the darkest valley, I fear no danger, for You are with me. Your rod and Your staff---they comfort me. You prepare a table before me in the presence of my enemies; You anoint my head with oil; my cup overflows. Only goodness and faithful love will pursue me all the days of my life, and I will dwell in the house of the Lord as long as I live." (Psalm 23)

R. S. V. P.

R. S. V. P. Does anybody really know what that means these days? I don't think so. I recently planned a special event at our church, asking . . . practically begging . . . for people to respond for the sake of planning. I sent out the R.S.V.P. request in writing; asked for it in spoken announcements and put it in the church bulletin. At the end of the day we expected over fifty and ended up with seventy-five. Now don't get me wrong, I was ecstatic to have seventy-five people in church to celebrate Advent at our Christmas Coffee House. There was plenty of food and more than enough seats, so it didn't present a problem. I'm just a worrier by nature . . . don't want anyone to arrive and not find a seat or miss that special piece of homemade pie. And in my typically naïve spirit, I really expected to have a better count, but alas, it was not to be. God used that experience to remind me of an urgent, life-changing message.

God sends out His invitation to us every day. He invites us to spend time with Him. He invites us to accept His living water. He invites us to pray and watch Him work. He invites us to make Him our Savior. But how many people never remember to R.S.V.P.? How many people place His divine invitation on the refrigerator with a cute magnet but never get around to answering His call? Is it because we forget or because life is just too busy and we don't take the time to "get back to Him"? Think about it. God has loved us since before we were formed in the womb, and He continues to love us and call us into relationship every single day. Some of us have answered his call for salvation, but we get careless about answering His *daily* call on our time, energy, and thoughts. Some of us have answered his call for relationship but allowed it to turn into legalistic religion. And some of us have simply put off answering Him at all, thinking that there's plenty of time to R.S.V.P. I'm here to say that time is running out. God does not *need* us, but He surely does *want* us to accept his invitation to be His children, to be servants in His kingdom, and to be saved by His grace.   He is the only one who can give us this amazing gift; we just have to R.S.V.P. and accept His outstretched hand.

'Répondez s'il vous plaît', to your gracious God today.   Don't let another moment go by without accepting His invitation of entering His presence and sitting at His feet. This R.S.V.P. doesn't even require a postage stamp; just a reverent, passionate acceptance of His forgiveness, grace and mercy. And what else comes along with your response? Joy...His true fullness of joy!

Ephesians 2:8-10, "For you are saved by grace through faith, and this is not from yourselves; it is God's gift --- not from works, so that no one can boast. For we are His creation, created in Christ Jesus for good works, which God prepared ahead of time so that we should walk in them."

Old Things

As long as I can remember, I have loved two things: flowers and "old stuff." I think there are some lessons for me in those items, lessons that are pretty telling about God and life. I guess the lessons of the flowers are pretty obvious; they are a poignant reminder of God's amazing creation. With every season, I never cease to be awed with the colors, shapes and varieties He provides and what an ingenious plan to have them spread their beauty over the year! Now the "old stuff" . . . that's another lesson.

I recall an Oprah Winfrey show I watched a few years ago and her decorator, Nate, completed a makeover that made me smile. He made over ugly basement walls with wood that had been salvaged from an old covered bridge. It was absolutely beautiful and the joy was that it was functional and indestructible as well. I started thinking about that wood this morning and I guess it's a lot like God's grace. He covers the ugly walls we've built up in our lives and with His grace, we become "more than conquerors," not to be defeated. Nate also said that the nature of the old wood keeps it from collecting dust. (I'm redoing my house tomorrow!) When we continue to abide in God's Word, hiding it in our hearts, we don't "collect dust" either. Now we may, like the wood, be full of blemishes and nicks, but we still look awfully good to God. That's because He loves us so much and sees what He can do with us, even when we're old and damaged. That old wood seems pretty plain . . . humble, if you will . . . compared to the new paneling and wallpapers on the market, but at the end of the day, it will outlast everything else. Aren't we like that? If we are willing to humble ourselves before God, His grace will be sufficient and we will be made strong through Him. For this, I am thankful, and I will never cease to praise Him and you know . . . I kind of like being "old wood." It just feels like home.

2 Corinthians 12:9-10, "But He said to me, "My grace is sufficient for you, for power is perfect in weakness." Therefore, I will most gladly boast all the more about my weaknesses, so that Christ's power may reside in me. So I take pleasure in weaknesses, insults, catastrophes, persecutions, and in pressures, because of Christ. For when I am weak, then I am strong."

One Word Can Change Everything

I have a plaque on the wall of what used to be my daughter, Whitney's room and it says this: "One shoe can change everything." ---Cinderella

I bought it for Whitney because she was the "Carrie Bradshaw" of our home, loving shoes like most people love breathing. (On a side note: now that she lives on her own, she has "tempered" her shoe craving. It's amazing what a budget will do) Anyway . . . I thought about that sign today as I did my homework for our latest women's Bible study at church: *Ruth: Loss, Love, and Legacy* (Kelly Minter). This study takes an incredibly slow look at the story of Ruth, dissecting its messages line by line, word by word. And do you know what? One **word** -- *not a shoe* – can change everything! Think about it.

Behold! – God's providence was at work for Ruth as she sought to take care of her mother-in-law, and this word also was used by the angels to announce the birth of Jesus.

Forgiveness – We are the righteousness of God because we are forgiven, having been bought by the blood of Jesus.

Grace – God gave the most amazing one-word gift of all: His grace.

Love – God's love for us is enough. The world will tell you that you need other things and people, but it's a lie. God's love is enough.

Finished – When Jesus said that it was finished (on the cross), He paved the way for our salvation and became the ultimate intercessor for us with God.

So, I am reminded of the power of a word. We can throw them around carelessly, leaving damaged goods in our paths. Or we can choose them carefully and lovingly, leaving blessing and stronger self-esteems as we go. I even think Cinderella would agree. She suffered from hurtful words that grew out of jealousy, and in the latter part of the story, she was blessed by a few words of a fairy godmother. Okay . . . the analogy ends there, but there *is* a point: our words can leave a legacy of love, goodness, and blessings for this generation and the next, and when we share *God's* words – grace, love, forgiveness – with others . . . well, behold! One word really can change everything!

Proverbs 18: 21, "Life and death are in the power of the tongue, and those who love it will eat its fruit."

Ephesians 4: 29, "No foul language is to come from your mouth, but only what is good for building up someone in need, so that it gives grace to those who hear."

Counting Fish

I don't have OCD, yet I feel the need to share this disclaimer up front since I'm about to admit something about myself that seems a little obsessive. I have a small fish pond right beside my deck. It's only four feet by six feet, but this miniature oasis gives me more joy than I can express. I bought the kit for myself for Mother's Day a number of years ago . . . BTW, that's the way to get what you want . . . I could do a seminar on this tactic. I asked my family to give me the "labor" as a gift. We started out with a handful of fish . . . goldfish, koi, the usual suspects and during the first winter, being the uninformed fish owner that I am, I was just sure they had all died from the cold. Well, no. They were doing what good fish do- hibernating. When they popped to the surface in the spring, I was shocked and thankful. Now the bad news is that in trying to be good fish parents, we cleaned too much, killing all but one of the first bunch. I guess ignorance is *not* bliss, especially if you're a fish in the Burden pond. Well, of course, we added more fish and since then our little habitat has thrived, despite my ignorant efforts to do the right thing but often missing the mark. So where does this story take its OCD turn?

A couple of seasons ago my fish started multiplying and I got ridiculously excited. Since then I have begun counting my fish on a daily basis. Yes, counting them. Now if you don't have an outside pond, you can't imagine how hard it is to accomplish this task. The little babies just don't stay still, no matter how much I coax them. In addition, our pond gets very green with algae and unless they are at the top, I can't really see them well. But, there is one time of day that I get to watch them and count with abandon: feeding time. My fish absolutely love to eat. They start swimming faster the moment they hear my feet on the deck. They rise to the top, knowing that Momma is approaching with breakfast and then the counting begins. Usually I change my visual angle and count more than once, especially if my number is off, meaning I can't see as many as I saw yesterday. This all started because I wanted to see if my babies were surviving and if my cats were using the pond for dinner; they have served themselves a "fish platter" from time to time and I even found a skeleton a few weeks ago. I also count because I just love seeing my little fish family growing before my very eyes, and in the counting yesterday, God gave me a Word.

I feel pretty silly with all of my counting, but God reminded me of a truth from His Word: He counts us, too. In the parable of the lost sheep in the book of Matthew, Jesus gives us a beautiful image of how much God loves the 99. However, He always keeps searching for the *one* who is lost, the *one* that has gone astray. He is never satisfied with 99%. God wants 100% of us living in relationship with Him and when he finds one stray fish, I mean, sheep . . . and brings it home, He rejoices! That's a pretty strong message. Our human hearts often get complacent when our percentage of success is above 95, telling ourselves that high percentages like that are the things of which success stories are made, but not God. He wants us *all --- every single one* of us --- no exceptions. He wants the woman who feels unworthy, the man who feels like a failure, the teen who has gone astray, the criminal who feels he can never be forgiven --- *every single one*. He is willing to search, to call out to us and wait patiently until we hear His voice and run to Him, whether we're running for the first time or returning after a visit in the far country. His prevenient grace woos us even before we know Him and His justifying grace makes us clean: "just-if-I'd" never done the stupid things I've done. Then He continues to sanctify us, drawing us closer and closer to Him, and bestowing His righteousness on us: the unworthy ones. He counts us, counts the hairs on our heads and counts our tears for one reason: He loves us and wants us in a relationship with Him – God – the Father of the universe. He counts us and, in addition, He is counting on us to return His love to Him first and then love others the way He has loved us.

As if that isn't enough good news, there's a really cool end to this OCD story. Yesterday my amazing husband of twenty-four years bought me an aquarium for our anniversary. Yes, I had already picked it out, priced it and told him which one to buy, but he got it done! I wanted this small version of my outdoor pond so I can continue to enjoy a few of my fish during the winter, something I've never been able to do before. Now counting won't be necessary in my aquarium, but this morning as I went out to feed the fish, do my daily counting, and pick a pair to bring into the house, I found something very exciting! There were not twelve...but *thirteen* fish. I was shocked, so I counted again and the number remained the same. Wow! I had felt that there were more than twelve, but since that's all I had seen in recent days, I couldn't be sure. I continued to do my faithful counting and this morning, it paid off: thirteen! This must be a very tiny glimpse of how God feels when He finds that last sheep and brings it home...content and glad He persisted, never giving up on the lost one.

I don't know about you, but I've been the "lost fish" before and I am overwhelmed with gratitude that God kept searching for me . . . counting until this one was found . . . and He is still counting.

Have you allowed Him to find you? And what are we, the body of Christ, doing to make sure the lost know Him today?

These are big questions that warrant our time, our prayers, our faithfulness, and our sacrifice. In the words of a favorite song, "Let it be said of us . . . that we would be joined as one body, that Christ would be seen by all." (Frye) What a privilege!

Luke 15: 3-7, "So He told them this parable: What man among you, who has 100 sheep and loses one of them, does not leave the 99 in the open field and go after the lost one until he finds it? When he has found it, he joyfully puts it on his shoulders and coming home, he calls his friends and neighbors together, saying to them, "Rejoice with me, because I have found my lost sheep!" I tell you, in the same way, there will be more joy in heaven over one sinner who repents than over 99 righteous people who don't need repentance."

Holding Fast

Hold fast - to hang on tightly, to cling tenaciously. That phrase seems to show up all over the place these days, so it must be a good one. Langston Hughes wrote about holding fast years ago, and I love his words. We must hold fast to our dreams so we don't have a life that is barren, unfulfilled, and broken. Good advice. Ulysses S. Grant wrote these words: "Hold fast to the Bible as the sheet anchor of your liberties. Write its precepts in your hearts, and practice them in your lives." The Christian group, Mercy Me, has written using that phrase, too, reminding us that we can't let go. Help *is* coming. More good advice: don't give up; be tenacious because God is coming at the exact right moment to save you . . . not a minute too soon or a minute too late . . . and in the meantime, He has you in His mighty grasp. Not just good advice but comfort as well.

Long before Mercy Me, Ulysses S. Grant, and Langston Hughes used this phrase, the writers of the Bible used it to tell us how to live. Need proof? Well, let me share...

Hebrews 10:23, "Let us hold fast the confession of our hope without wavering, for He who promised is faithful."

Hebrews 10:35, "Therefore do not cast away (hold fast to . . . my paraphrase) your confidence, which has great reward."

Romans 12:9, "Let love be without hypocrisy. Abhor what is evil. Cling to (hold fast to . . . me again) what is good."

2 Thessalonians 2:15, "Therefore, brethren, stand fast and hold the traditions which you were taught, whether by word or our epistle."

Hebrews 4:14-16, "Seeing then that we have a great High Priest who has passed through the heavens, Jesus the Son of God, let us hold fast our confession. For we do not have a High Priest who cannot sympathize with our weaknesses, but was in all points tempted as we are, yet without sin. Let us therefore come boldly to the throne of grace that we may obtain mercy and find grace to help in time of need."

Okay, so we should hold fast to . . . our dreams, God's Word, God's grasp, good things, our hope, our traditions and our confession of Jesus as Lord and Savior. Is this worth holding fast? I surely believe it is and I will cling tenaciously to God because, in the words of Mercy Me, "Help is on the way!"

Epilogue: There is a repeated pattern in my life that has occurred in the last few years. If God wants to make a point either with me or through me for someone else, He shows me that very thing three times in a row. I know it sounds crazy, but the pattern has surfaced over and over, and I have written these times in my journals . . . just to document the wonder of it all! Yesterday I wrote this devotional because it had been on my heart. Then this morning, I read and heard it two more times. Coincidence? No. A "God wink," if I may borrow the phrase coined by Squire Rushnell in his book of the same name (*When God Winks at You: How God Speaks Directly to You Through the Power of Coincidence*, 2006). So there's a point He obviously wants us to remember.

We simply *must* hold fast to our confidence in God, and that very confidence has great reward. He is aching to bless us, just as earthly parents love to bless their children. He wants us to experience His greatest rewards, but to have what He desires so much to give, we **MUST** hold fast to our confidence in Him . . . our confidence that He has overcome the world, our confidence that He has a good plan for our lives, our confidence that He walks with us through "the valley of the shadow of death," our confidence that no matter what our circumstances look like right now, He works everything . . . I said

EVERYTHING . . . out for good for those who love Him. Don't miss this. I didn't say that everything *is* good; I said He works everything out *for* good, but you must hold fast to your confidence in His love, His power, and His goodness. I wish I could say these things to you in person today because I am feeling them with a passion that He obviously has put in my heart, but since I'm here and you're there (wherever you are, Sisters and Brothers . . .), listen to these words and believe them. God didn't give them to me by accident. He has "winked" at us this morning, and like the light He created in Genesis, it is *very* good.

"But test all things; hold on to what is good." (1 Thessalonians 5:17)

Figaro's Mess

It's amazing what we can learn when we truly pay attention to God's Word and actually do what it says. Yesterday was one of those times when I *really* got it . . . and it involved cleaning up a nasty mess.

A week ago, I "took back" my favorite room in our home: the sun porch. When I say that I "took it back," I mean that I rescued it from the dust, the dirt that had tumbled from the plants, the leaves that had fallen, and the mess I had allowed to build up over time . . . the mess that always builds up when school gets the best of me. It was such a joy to sit out there last weekend, reading, rocking and praying in that clean, peaceful space again. But the pleasure was short-lived.

Somehow, without realizing it, we allowed Figaro, the kitten, to slip into the porch unnoticed. If you've followed my devotionals, you've heard of her before. She seems to get into all kinds of trouble! After a long day at work, followed by a ballgame, I came home to hear her distant cry and found her in my porch . . . needless to say, *NOT* a clean porch anymore. She had dumped the plants to use the dirt for a litter box. She had knocked trinkets off the shelves and made a general wreck of things. I was tempted at first to be upset, but in Jake's (my youngest son) words of wisdom, I was reminded that it wasn't her fault. She didn't mean to make a mess; she just found herself caught in a bad situation, locked in a room without food or water, with no way out. The following Saturday morning I gathered my cleaning supplies and started the process over again, not happily at first. However, it wasn't long before I was reminded of the scripture that tells us to do everything . . . *all work* . . . as unto the Lord.

"Really?" I asked God. Yes, really. He didn't just mean the jobs that we like or the ones that suit our fancy. He didn't just mean the easy jobs or the ones that give us lots of glory. He means *all* jobs, and when we work as unto the Lord, it's amazing how an attitude can change in a single moment.

I swept, scrubbed, picked up, and washed the things she dirtied. I mopped, dusted, and put plants out on the deck for some fresh air, and yes, I did it with joy and a smile on my face. Not my norm for housework, but something to which I aspire. And it's amazing: God gave me a Word while I was working. Isn't He wonderful like that? When we take the right attitude and spirit into our work, He can then reward us with a Word from the Almighty. So here's the Word I needed, and maybe you need it, too.

We make a myriad of messes in our lives and end up in the metaphorical "pits," in the words of Beth Moore. Some of the pits we dig ourselves, and we jump right in. Sometimes we're thrown in by others and at other times we slip in accidentally, like Figaro whose presence in the porch wasn't her fault. No matter the kind of pit, we still find ourselves bogged down in miry clay, but God always finds a way. When we're willing to return to Him, He help's us clean up our messes. He doesn't say we have to clean up *before* we come to Him; He just says, "Come." And when He cleans our "porch," we are totally clean, like the mess never happened. This is what His justifying grace is all about: we are justified through Christ, "just-if-I'd" never made the mess in the first place. My porch is that way today: totally clean, like Figaro never wrought havoc. So where is she now? She's still trying to slip into the porch so she can stay close to me . . . the one who loves her even when she's a mess. That's where I want to be, close to God who loves me unconditionally and justifies me by His amazing grace.

If you have a mess in your life, it's never hopeless because, with God, all things are possible. He can and will lift you out of the miry clay and set your feet upon a rock: the rock of Jesus Christ, the Savior of the world. Just ask Him, and be tenacious in the asking. And what's more . . . He will do it with the joy of the Lord!

Figaro's Rescue

Inspiration comes from the strangest places, and yesterday was no exception. I am a cat lover and a rescuer, and those two pieces of me came together in a proverbial need-the-fire-department-ladder moment. I went out to feed my cats, and there was one kitten I could hear but not see: Figaro. I searched high and low . . . and then high again . . . and there she was – perched on a small twig at the end of a limb in a large gum tree. She was scared, clinging, and way beyond my reach, even with a ladder. I moved my car underneath her (in case she fell) and called her repeatedly. No luck. She was simply too scared to move. Finally I went inside, only to go back out later and find her on a more stable limb, a little closer to the trunk. Progress.

To make a long story short, after calling her name, standing on the rail of my husband's "man cave," and begging her to come down, it occurred to me to put a board against the tree. She trusted me enough to jump onto the board, and Figaro was saved. But you know there's a point to this mundane, stereotypical cat story.

As I stood on the rail of the man cave, calling her name repeatedly, I saw a clear image of God's grace. I called her name in my gentlest voice, begging her to make her way back to me from the small dangerous twig. I continued calling her name when she seemed to be desperate to make her way toward my voice. I reached out my hand to her, trying to woo her to come to me, even though she was scared to death . . . a real "scaridy cat" (bad joke). I never stopped calling, and I kept looking for a solution to her situation; I just wanted her to come "home," so to speak . . . to jump into my arms. Isn't God like that?

God calls us back to Him from the far country, or the far "limb" of life. He loves us, whispers our names, and reaches His hand out to us when we are afraid, crying out, and scared to death. With His amazing grace, He loves us even when we're on the other side of the tree and we can't see Him: He *always* sees us, and He never stops wanting us to make our way back to Him and His safety. Sometimes He even offers us a "board," a place to land when we need to come home. And, if we find ourselves on a shaky limb again...He still loves us, reaches out to us and offers us His rescue.

Amazing grace . . . *very* amazing

How did the story end? I hugged Figaro, and she clung to my shoulder. I blocked the porch door so she could get in and out and rest in a place of safety while Dan and I went out of town. I provided food and water and gave her time to re-nourish herself in my safety zone. Again, the metaphor can't be missed: "The Lord is my shepherd; I shall not want. He makes me lie down in green pastures. He leads me beside still waters. He restores my soul." I am awed by His amazing grace, and I am blessed to hear Him calling me, wooing me every day into His omnipotent arms of blessing.

If you are afraid or lost or in need of a Savior today, be a Figaro: jump on that board and run to God. He never stops calling your name, and He will celebrate when you let Him be the Father He longs to be. Abba . . . Father . . . no greater love than this.

"Yahweh your God is among you, a warrior who saves. He will rejoice over you with gladness. He will bring you quietness with His love. He will delight in you with shouts of joy." (Zephaniah 3:17)

My Love Language

Anybody ever read the book about love languages? It's an interesting and spot-on book that explains how we, as humans, all speak different love languages. The language that speaks to me is not necessarily the language that speaks to my spouse. It's an eye-opening text that helps the reader realize how he/she needs to communicate differently with others because they speak a different love language.

God understands this, too.

This morning I woke up because my 17-year old cat, Charlie, thought it was time to eat. She was nudging me, mewing loudly and refusing to be denied. So, I got up. And no sooner had I headed to the kitchen than a song slipped quietly into my brain: "Beneath the Cross of Jesus." I haven't heard it recently and haven't thought of it, so I know God was speaking. He knows my love languages with Him, and my strongest one is music. And so He speaks through song.

I love it when He does this because I know there's something to be noticed, something to be studied, something to be gained. If He takes the time and care to speak to me in my language, I need to pay attention and so I did.

Here are those lyrics, penned in 1868 by Elizabeth Clephane and published posthumously. I think it's poignant that the words were first shared in a magazine entitled *Breathing on the Border*. Perfect.

Beneath the cross of Jesus I fain would take my stand,
The shadow of a mighty rock within a weary land;
A home within the wilderness, a rest upon the way,
From the burning of the noontide heat and the burden of the day.

O safe and happy shelter, O refuge tried and sweet,
O trysting place where Heaven's love and Heaven's justice meet!
As to the holy patriarch that wondrous dream was given,
So seems my Savior's cross to me, a ladder up to heaven.

There lies beneath its shadow but on the further side
The darkness of an awful grave that gapes both deep and wide
And there between us stands the cross two arms outstretched to save
A watchman set to guard the way from that eternal grave.

Upon that cross of Jesus mine eye at times can see
The very dying form of One Who suffered there for me;
And from my stricken heart with tears two wonders I confess;
The wonders of redeeming love and my unworthiness.

I take, O cross, thy shadow for my abiding place;
I ask no other sunshine than the sunshine of His face;
Content to let the world go by to know no gain or loss,
My sinful self my only shame, my glory all the cross.

Were you surprised, like I was, to find verses that we don't normally sing in church? Maybe this is why God spoke to me with song this morning: there's a powerful message in stanza 3:

There lies beneath its shadow but on the further side
The darkness of an awful grave that gapes both deep and wide
And there between us stands the cross two arms outstretched to save
A watchman set to guard the way from that eternal grave

Did you read it carefully? There is an awful grave, both deep and wide, waiting for each and every one of us. It's inevitable. Whether I die today, or tomorrow, death is coming and the grave is not a pleasant image I like to ponder. But God offers us a way out: between us and that grave stands the cross . . . the Cross of Christ, "two arms outstretched to save" us. We don't have to walk straight into that grave, and even better, we can look forward to the day we go there because God has provided another way: Jesus Christ, His only Son.

But here's the problem: if you don't know Him, then the grave is all you have in your future. If your friends don't know Him . . . if your co-workers don't know Him . . . if your family members don't know Him . . . if your neighbors don't know Him . . . the grave is all there is. Are you willing to take that chance with the people you love? Don't they deserve to know that the grave is not the end?

In John 3:16, a very familiar verse, it says this: "God so loved the world that He gave His only begotten Son, that whosoever believes in Him should not perish but have everlasting life." *Whosoever. The whole world.* God is not in the business of exclusivity. He wants everyone to know Him, accept His Son as Lord and Savior and live with Him in eternity. What an amazing, open offer to the world! We don't have to perish; we can live with Him eternally. Why would we want anything else for ourselves and our loved ones and, indeed, for the whole world?

We have a responsibility to do what Jesus commanded, to go to all nations and tell the world that He is Lord. And "all nations" starts at home, in our neighborhood, and in our community. *All nations . . .* everyone deserves to know that the end isn't the end. We can't keep it a secret or act like it isn't the incredible good news that it is. We must live in such a way that others want our faith. We must use our messes to share a message of hope with others. We must use our tests and trials to glorify God. We must go and tell.

I think it's perfect that this beautiful poem was published in a magazine called *Breathing on the Border.* Isn't that what we are doing today as believers? We are still breathing on the border of death, but the difference for us and others is this: we are breathing on the border of *heaven,* waiting for the day when we see Jesus face to face. I don't even see the grave anymore because it won't hold me. It has no meaning in my life. And when my day comes to go there, I will celebrate because I will breathe on the other side, kneeling before my God and singing like never before. Hallelujah!

Momma's Table

There are memories that are forever etched in the deep recesses of our minds. As the brain would have it, they are usually connected to incredibly pleasant experiences or deeply painful ones. In this case, the memory is comfortable and melancholy, and it centers on a not-so special table in a small dining room in a sleepy Southern town.

In the world's estimation, my parents didn't have very much. Their house was small with one heater in the center and I don't mean central heat, and one window air conditioning unit. It was always a Carrier. Was there anything else? They had no credit cards and no fancy cars and my sisters and I grew up without vehicles and privilege. But we had something much better and I can see it so clearly now that I am older looking back on it: we had Godly parents and a table full of love. My mother had a small, nondescript dining room table and when it got too small for the family, my daddy bought a piece of plywood. He was no handyman, but he managed to put the plywood on top of the table to make it bigger. Momma bought a soft piece of padding, added a table cloth and overnight, she had a bigger "table." When it was not being used for meals, we removed the cloths, added a net and played ping pong. I know my mother must have bit through her lip from time to time as she tolerated our playing ping pong in her little dining room, but I never heard her complain. Anyway, back to the table...

We ate Sunday lunch at my mother's house at 215 Elizabeth Street every single week. Always more food than we could eat . . . two meats, scalloped potatoes, macaroni and cheese baked long enough to form perfect crunchy cheese on the edges, hot banana pudding . . . food fit for Southern kings and queens, and we loved it. After the meal, there was a lot of "sitting around," just sitting, visiting and talking. I can't even remember the topics of conversation, but I remember sitting there for hours. In her later years, my mother loved staying dressed in her pastel blue or pink silky pajamas and robe and I can still see her sitting at that table dressed in just that way. One foot tucked under her, drinking a tall glass of iced tea, not rushing to clear the table. We spent a lot of time at that table and it struck me just recently that the peace and joy found at momma's makeshift table is so very similar to what God wants to give us.

 In the devotional book *At His Feet*, Chris Tiegreen writes this: "In the dining room of our life, He wants the lengthy personal fellowship of the common meal, not the brief acknowledgement before it."

God wants us to feast in His presence and hang around with Him long after the "meal." He wants us to laugh, cry, talk and listen. He wants us to sit down with Him to dine on His Word, enjoy the sweetness of His love, and learn from His wisdom. But in this fast paced society, we too often give ourselves over to more than we should do and somehow, we lose the belief that we have time to sit still in His presence. It's a lie from the greatest of all liars: Satan. He wants us to believe that being busy, even for God, is what God always intended, but it's simply not true.

Read God's Word – the Truth of all truths – and you will find that God wants us to "lie down in green pastures" and rest "beside still waters." He wants to "restore our souls." To be restored, we must sit still at God's great dining table of worship and love Him. In Isaiah, it says that if we wait on the Lord, we will renew our strength, rising to soar like eagles. In January, I intend to do a lot of waiting on God, sitting at His table of mercy and grace, listening to His voice, and cherishing the comfort of a place where I can be still and visit without rushing to "clean up" my life or do another chore. I want to do with God what I wish I could do with my mother, who I lost to cancer over 27 years ago: I want to pour my praises on Him, thanking Him for the profound and immeasurable blessings He has poured into my life. I pray that you will choose to spend extended time at His table, allowing His love to wash over you like the aroma of home-made biscuits from a Southern woman's kitchen.

My older son, Asher, recently enabled us to have a very large dining room table for the first time in our married life. It can seat up to twelve and we are already creating our own family memories. We may not solve the world's problems this year or figure out the economy, but we will surely create some very good table memories, and maybe, just maybe, one day, my children and grandchildren will remember that at Grandma and Poppa's table, they were loved . . . truly loved.

Psalm 23:1-3, "The LORD is my shepherd, I lack nothing. He makes me lie down in green pastures, he leads me beside quiet waters, He refreshes my soul."

Psalm 46:10, "Be still, and know that I am God."

Learning and Loving It

I love learning. I don't think I always knew that fact, but I do now. I love to learn new songs, read new books and learn new ways of doing things. I love Pinterest because it is helping me learn to be a better cook and I didn't think that was possible! Bottom line: I love to learn and I especially love learning God's Word. Recently I heard a sermon that showed me some familiar scriptures and yet opened my eyes to new knowledge.

"Moses then took the blood, sprinkled it on the people and said, "This is the blood of the covenant that the LORD has made with you in accordance with all these words." (Exodus 24:8)

I have read this many times, but until I heard this particular sermon, I never noticed that the blood was not just sprinkled on the altar; it was sprinkled on the *people*. This was the old covenant that God sealed with the people through Moses and the people were covered with the blood of the sacrifice. Today, we are covered with the blood of Jesus' sacrifice. His blood seals the new covenant God made with His people and in the words of the old hymn, "There is power in the blood."

A-ha #2: Moses had to wait on God often. In Exodus 24, we are told that Moses went up the mountain but God did not speak until the seventh day. How often do we pray and expect God to move immediately? The truth is that God speaks in *His* timing and His timing is always perfectly planned for His kingdom. I can be terribly impatient and I sometimes move ahead of Him, but He always pulls me back and then I am reminded to wait on Him and His voice.

A-ha #3: God told Moses to tell the people to give their offerings to build a sanctuary – a holy place – where He could reside. Today we don't need to build a physical sanctuary, but we surely need to create a holy place in our hearts where God can live. We need to repent, allowing God to cleanse our hearts and create newness in us. We need to study His Word, keeping it in our hearts so it becomes the driving force of our thinking and our living. We need to give Him every space and every piece of ourselves, allowing Him to inhabit the secret places of our souls. It is in giving Him the sanctuary of ourselves, His holy temple, that our lives will honor and glorify God, the Father.

And this is what I love about reading God's Word and attending Bible study – we can look at something we've seen a hundred times and yet when we see it with a fresh perspective, there is so much to gain. The Bible is never dated and never wrong and I know that if you will commit to living in His Word, you will see Him with fresh eyes and a new joy.

Psalm 119:105, "Your Word is a lamp to my feet and a light to my path."

Be a Pig, Not a Chicken

I was asked an interesting question a few days ago: do you ever do anything that's outside the Bible? I thought for a moment, and my answer was, "I sure hope not." But that question has forced me to think about my life and the witness I live before others. Am I more than a bumper sticker?

The principal at my school, Judy Beard, loves to repeat a simple but powerful little story about a farm and breakfast. When you think of breakfast foods, what's the greatest difference between the pig and the chicken? The chicken is involved; the pig is committed.

Are we pigs or chickens for Christ?

It's simple, really. Are we involved in church, going to services and singing the songs and even serving on committees, but not really living out the command of Jesus to love others . . . the least of these? Or are we totally committed? Do people see us and know beyond a shadow of a doubt that we live for Christ, loving others the way He did? Do they feel God's love when they talk to me? Do they see me as a person who loves the unlovable . . . unconditionally? Or do they see me talk the talk but never walk the walk?

This is serious business.

I heard one of my pastors say recently that in this country we have somehow ceased to be committed. He was planting the spiritual seeds of going on a mission trip outside the United States. In his words, "Go to another country and serve. You will be smitten, and you will never be the same when you return." I feel sure he is right. Seeing people who have never been told of Jesus --- seeing people who live in abject poverty and yet seek something more --- seeing people who are willing to worship in secret because they have learned the power of serving Christ --- that would definitely transform complacent church attendance into a greater appreciation of grace. Commitment breeds commitment.

I am a middle school teacher and in my school, we are pigs. We have an extraordinary leader who lives to serve children. She is innovative in her thinking and doing and children benefit every time she breaks an old barrier of learning. I love working beside her because she is committed to the children of our city; we share the same heart and her commitment bolsters mine, especially on the days when I am tired and a little discouraged. Commitment is contagious and uplifting.

And so I'm back to the question: are we going to be chickens, involved in the task at hand but not completely committed? Or are we willing to be pigs, fully invested in the Lord's work and His kingdom? When I ponder this, I think of a writer who says He wants to not only know God, but to be known as belonging to Him. That's my desire as well. I want everyone to know that I belong completely to Christ, not just when I write and sing, but when I live every single day. I want every action and decision to be measured against the perfect example of my Savior. I want to wear a cross around my neck and live like the Cross changed my life because it did. Will I fail sometimes? Yes. I am a sinner, but I am committed to a Savior who forgives and expects me to forgive others in return. I do that quickly and gratefully because of what He did for me.

Have you deeply pondered God's grace lately? Spend time in His presence, remembering the things He has done for you. Re-commit yourself to Him and Him alone, letting His dedication to a relationship with you be the driving force that carries you every single day.

Be more than a bumper sticker. Be a pig.

Galatians 2:20, "I have been crucified with Christ; it is no longer I who live, but Christ lives in me; and the life which I now live in the flesh I live by faith in the Son of God, who loved me and gave Himself for me."

Part II: Being a Pig

The government may shut down. The debt ceiling may break into a million tiny little pieces. And chemical weapons might not be put away. These things are important; I get it, but I also get something else this morning: the issues we are dealing with spiritually in this country and in my own community trump all of those issues in my heart and mind.

If the government shuts down, my God will not. He is still on the throne, guiding us, calling to us and waiting with open arms to bless us. God has not retired.

If the economy crashes again, my God will not. He is not broke and He always provides. In His economy, things don't look bleak; they look hopeful.

If people choose to kill each other --- and they will --- God is still omnipotent God and He will do whatever He must to avenge all wrongs in the world. I am not in charge, and you are not in charge; God is in charge and He has told us to let Him be our mighty avenger.

This morning I am tired of the "big" news of the day when the things right in my sphere of influence need my prayers and my loving attention.

I am worried about the young man who is hungry every afternoon before he leaves school. I will feed him, love him and pray for him.

I am worried about the young men and women in my school who are reading below grade level and may not be able to get a diploma or a well-paying job in the future. They need to be able to take care of their families, and it worries me that they will not be able to do what they dream. I will tutor them, read with them and pray for them that their minds will turn on to learning and knowledge.

I am worried about people I love who don't know Christ and don't know His mighty power and unexplainable peace. I will pray for them, love them and live before them as an example.

I am worried about the church at large. We have not always done the job God deserves of following the model of Jesus and it has turned a generation away from Christ. I talk to people who want nothing to do with the church because, in their minds, it represents exclusion and judgment. They have closed their hearts to the God and the Christ I serve --- a Christ who loved all people and hung out with them because they needed Him. He ran to the sinners, eating dinner with them and meeting them where they were. Our world is hungry for a church that will do that today. I will open my doors and my arms to those who need Christ most.

Today I will choose to act and pray --- not worry. I will choose to love and meet needs --- not sit in my pristine world and take care of only my needs. Today I will be a pig, not a bumper sticker, committed wholly and unashamedly to the cause of Christ. I will cry out to God and He will hear my prayers, not because it is me but because He has promised to answer our cries and hold our tears in the palm of His hands. I will trust Him today and live for Him only.

Spaces in the Heart

On the wall of my study/grandchildren's play room is a sign that reads, "Grandchildren fill a space in your heart that you never knew was empty." My daughter, Meredith, gave me the sign as a gift, but the even greater gift is her precious daughter, Olivia, who talks to me on FaceTime, squealing when she sees me and hears my voice. I have five other amazing, beautiful grandchildren that continue to fill the spaces of my heart as well. There's Chandler, the token male, bless his heart! Then there's our precocious Hannah who is already learning to be a little momma at seven years old. Hannah's best pal is little sister, Addelyn, a miracle of birth and a blessing to all of us. To round out the crowd, there is Lily Grace, another miracle of God's grace, and our own little bulldozer, Harper, who is determined to use her legs to their fullest, now that she has learned how to be mobile. Before these precious babies were born into our already large family, I was very content. I have a crowd of sons and daughters and I love them all dearly. But you see...the sign is right, these grandchildren have filled a space I didn't realize I had. My love has multiplied exponentially because of their birth into our family.

There's another empty space in our hearts that can't be filled with children, or spouses, work, or possessions. It's a God-sized hole and He is the only peg that fits. And the difference in this empty space and the one my grandchildren fill? We know it's there. We may not admit it, but oh yes, we know very well.

I see people every day trying to fill the holes in their hearts. They don't say that's what they are doing, but I can see it. They are building bigger houses than anyone could possibly need. They are buying better toys and more impressive cars, sometimes when those cherished items create overwhelming debt. Many are filling themselves with alcohol or drugs or more food than a body is designed to hold, while still others are staying way too busy just to avoid being alone. So why do we do it?

There's a simple answer:

We *know* there's a hole in our hearts. We sense it and we scramble to fill it. But that hole has only one peg that will fit . . . only one puzzle piece with all of the right edges. That piece is God.

God designed us to be in relationship with Him. He tells us in Scripture that we are made in His image. And since that is true, it only makes sense to be in relationship with another after whom we are modeled. Without that relationship in place, nothing else in our puzzle of life seems to fit. Hence, the junk we use in a desperate attempt to fill that gigantic hole.

It will never work. Never has and never will.

Years ago I tried to fill that hole, quite unsuccessfully I might add. I accepted relationships that were not healthy for me. I worked frantically in an attempt to keep the people around me happy. What a joke! I started my day early and ended it very late all in an attempt to keep myriad balls in the air, but at the end of the day, the balls crashed and I found myself wondering what went wrong.

I thank God that, in His grace and mercy, He didn't stop seeking me. I was the lost prodigal who desperately needed to come home and fill the spaces of her heart with the only thing that works and lasts.

Am I still busy? You better believe it, but here's the difference. I have allowed God, my Father and Jesus, the Savior of my life, to guide my choices. As I told someone just yesterday, I have a very full life, but I only give my time, energy and talents to the endeavors God has chosen for me . . . the passions of my life. I have asked God, who has filled the hole in my heart to overflowing, to change my desires to His desires and so I give myself to those tasks with passion and zeal. In other words, if I'm not passionate about it and designed by God for it, I probably don't do it.

It's a simpler way to live and one that creates joy, peace and fulfillment.

I don't try to fill my heart with the approval of people who would judge me; I try to live every day to honor God and love Him openly and I accept the rest. Will everyone be pleased with me? Probably not, but as long as God is pleased, I am more than fine.

No more scrambling, no more acts of desperation to feel worthy. Not necessary . . . the hole is filled.

Lift your heart, your hands and your empty spaces to God today. He will be faithful to welcome you home and fill the well of your heart with His love. What a way to overflow!

Romans 5:5, "This hope will not disappoint us, because God's love has been poured out in our hearts through the Holy Spirit who was given to us."

Reach Out and Touch

I am a hugger. I feel sure it must be in my DNA because I've been a hugger as long as I can remember. I hug my family, I hug my students, I hug my dog, Belle, every morning, and I even hug strangers when we meet. Maybe it's partially because I'm a Southerner through and through, and hugging is part of my hospitality, but I think it's more than that. Hugging is my way of making people feel loved, accepted, welcomed, and sometimes, forgiven. Hugging is healing because it's about touching people in a healthy, positive way. I've been thinking a lot about this lately . . . this idea of the power of human touch, and God's Word has a lot to say about it, too.

In reading the Gospels, we see over and over that Jesus healed people who touched Him. The woman with years of bleeding simply reached out to touch the hem of His garment, and she was healed immediately. In another passage, Jesus touched the eyes of a blind man, and he received his sight. In Luke 6, it says this: "And the people all tried to touch him, because power was coming from him and healing them all." People knew the power of touching Jesus. They reached out to Him in faith because they knew that one touch from Him would heal their diseases. But there's more.

The power of a touch from Jesus can do way more for us than just heal our physical bodies; Jesus reaches in and touches our souls, and when He does, we are never the same. In the song "He Touched Me" (by Bill Gaither) it says that "something happened" because of Jesus' touch. I can't explain exactly what it is that happens when Jesus touches our souls, but I know this: when we have a "touching" encounter with our Savior, we are never, ever the same again. He begins to transform our lives and our thinking. He heals our hearts of damage and pain. He causes us to look on others differently. One touch from a Savior, and the metamorphosis begins.

But here's the problem: touching Jesus means we have to seek Him and spend time with Him. It can't just be a casual 5-minute encounter. Seeking Jesus' touch means we need to sit at the foot of the Cross and ask for His healing hand to be upon us. It means we need to kneel before the throne and bow humbly before our Savior. It means we need to put everything else aside and reach our hands out to Jesus . . . to grab His hand or simply touch the hem of His garment or the tassels of His robe. We have to *want* to be touched and healed, and we must seek intimacy with Him. It's not like He's hard to find; He is waiting to touch our hearts and our lives because He desires to bless us.

This isn't complicated, so why do people not seek Him?

Seeking takes sacrifice. Seeking takes time. Seeking means putting other things aside or away to give total focus to our Lord. Seeking means pursuing with a holy obsession. And most people don't want to give Him everything. They want a quick touch and no more because more requires sacrifice.

Is there anything worth holding onto that is in the way of your receiving a meaningful touch from the Savior? I don't think so.

I encourage and implore you today to sit with Jesus. Reach out for His hand and don't let go. Refuse to walk alone, knowing He desires to walk your journey with you, every step of the way. Ask Him for a touch to heal the places in your heart and body that need restoration. Sit at His feet and let Him wrap you in His arms. You will find healing, peace, and joy to flood your soul!

Today and in the days to come, I will see myself worshiping at the manger and worshiping at His mercy seat. I will see myself touching that bed of straw and holding His gentle but mighty hand. I will see healing in Him that can be found nowhere else, and I will be thankful. And obsessed? Yes, I will be obsessed with the touch of my Savior.

Oh, glorious day!

Luke 8: 43-48,   And a woman was there who had been subject to bleeding for twelve years,[a] but no one could heal her. 44 She came up behind him and touched the edge of his cloak, and immediately her bleeding stopped.

45 "Who touched me?" Jesus asked.

When they all denied it, Peter said, "Master, the people are crowding and pressing against you."

46 But Jesus said, "Someone touched me; I know that power has gone out from me."

47 Then the woman, seeing that she could not go unnoticed, came trembling and fell at his feet. In the presence of all the people, she told why she had touched him and how she had been instantly healed. 48 Then he said to her, "Daughter, your faith has healed you. Go in peace."

Staying Power or When Willpower Fails

I've been pondering a lot lately about why I have trouble sticking to certain things. Certain things like diets . . . it drives me crazy. I'm in that stage of life when weight has become more of an issue than it used to be and though my mind *wants* to be the size I was two years ago, my hand keeps moving toward my mouth with food that definitely isn't on my current eating plan. Every time I go to the closet and something I want to wear doesn't fit over my hips ☹...I promise myself to stick to the plan all day. Invariably, someone at work shows up with a homemade chocolate chip cookie and my flesh takes over. Is it mind over matter? Is it weak willpower? Or do I just love food more than I love being smaller? My mother once said, "I don't have an emotional eating disorder, I just love to eat!" I'm in total agreement, and it makes it incredibly difficult to stick to the healthy eating plan I've adopted. So how does this relate to my relationship with God?

In our spiritual lives, we don't have to depend on willpower; we have to depend on God. But even then, we have to be diligent in asking Him to help us focus our hearts and minds on Him. In Isaiah 26:3, it says this: **"You will keep him in perfect peace whose mind is stayed on You because he trusts in You."** So don't we all want perfect peace? Peace that is beyond what the world can understand? I sure do, but the only way to have that state of true tranquility in the midst of the storms of life is to keep our minds on God --- *stick* with Him --- every day, all day. We can't just pray a quick prayer in the morning and forget Him the rest of the day. In the words of Scripture, we must "pray without ceasing" and I used to think that was impossible, but *nothing* is impossible with God.

Here are a few thoughts for sticking to God – mind, heart and spirit:

- Ask God every morning to help you seek His face.

- Place scriptures on index cards in strategic places (your refrigerator, the dashboard of your car, in the bathroom, in your purse, on your desk).

- Ask God to make you want more of Him.

- Play K-Love or another Christian music station in your car.

- Play the Christian Contemporary music channel on your TV when you're at home. (Great for house cleaning)

- Fast for a day. You can fast food, TV . . . anything that helps you focus on God and seek Him throughout the day.

There are more ways to turn toward Him, but these are a few places to get started. Years ago, I began with changing the radio station in my car and it rechanneled my entire focus because it kept me thinking about Him as I headed into work. Today I listen to the radio less and ride in silence more . . . talking to Him as I head into another challenging day and still I fail sometimes. But there is always more grace than failures and God continues to seek me, "wooing" me into more and more time with Him. He wants that with *all* of us. Listen as He calls your name and stick with Him more and more. Your life will be transformed and you *will* be able to live in the perfect peace only He provides. Perfect.

1 Thessalonians 5:16-18, "Rejoice always, pray without ceasing, give thanks in all circumstances, for this is the will of God in Christ Jesus for you."

The Doctrine of More

In the United States, we seem to always want more . . . more money, more exciting experiences, more things to fill our already cluttered houses, more space to put the stuff we collect, more food, more love...more, more, more. It never seems to end. People are filling their lives with the things that are comfortable, fun, and maybe even showy, but in the end, these things won't last. When we are gone from the earth, we can't take those things, and where has our money gone? I'd be willing to bet that most of us have attics and "spare rooms" full of the "more" we just had to have and now find it to be in our way. This is the stuff of yard sales and visits to Good Will. The stuff we thought we couldn't live without, but there's another way to look at "more."

I recently heard a pastor use this phrase, "the doctrine of more". Only, she didn't mean more possessions; she shared that God has so much more in store for us than we even know. Her phrase snagged my heart and it reminded me of another image shared long ago.

Another pastor explained it this way: when we die, God will open a door in heaven, showing us rooms of unopened presents. These are the blessings we could have received if we had been open to God's voice and His amazing grace, but because we weren't in a true, deep relationship with Him, our Creator and Father, many of those gifts were left unopened. More blessings we could have received. Wow.

Just to clarify, I do believe God blesses us every day in ways we didn't even ask for, but the problem is this: with God, we can always have more. More grace, more joy, more peace, more love, more comfort, more strength, more perseverance, more forgiveness, more blessings. We just need to talk to Him, love Him, and delight in Him. We need to thank Him for every single "present," both large and small. We must spend time with Him daily, and love Him supremely, making Him our priority. He is our Father, just waiting to bless us with His goodness.

And yet, we often get too busy or too wrapped up in ourselves to open the floodgate of those amazing blessings. What a shame.

My daddy used to love to buy me gifts. He would take my sisters and me shopping for dresses or special items we wanted, and even when I became an adult, he loved to buy me blue jeans. Yes, blue jeans. You see, my daddy had no sons, and he is a died-in-the-wool outdoorsman. He loved to see his girls in blue jeans. I finally told him that I could only wear so many pairs, so we agreed to switch to something I *really* wanted: some of his collection of Case knives. Well, what a floodgate! He began to buy me beautifully crafted Case knives, but more special than that, he gave me many of his old knives and these are the ones that mean the most to me now. I remember asking him, "Daddy, are you sure you want to give these to me now? You can wait until later because I know you love them." His response was that of a perfect father and gift-giver. He said, "Honey, I want you to have them right now so you can enjoy them and I can see your delight in getting them while I'm still alive." He is such a wise and loving man, formed in the image and heart of God, our heavenly Father. And just like God, my daddy wanted me to have the best gifts right now so he could see me enjoy them and put them to use in positive ways. I believe this is what God wants as well.

God wants to bless us richly. He can do unimaginable things in our lives if we will invite Him into our daily moments. I also believe that He relishes watching us enjoy the amazing blessings He provides. And when we use our blessings to glorify Him, He surely must smile, just as my daddy beamed with pride when I got excited about every single knife.

Today, I implore you to sit with your Father. Talk with Him, giving Him your whole heart. Love Him above all else and listen to Him. You might even pray the prayer of Jabez, as I do every day with a few added words (Jean's paraphrase!): "Lord, please bless me indeed, and enlarge my territory for *Your* Kingdom and *Your* glory. Keep evil from me, that I might walk in *Your* ways all day." Delight in Him, and let Him bless you beyond measure, giving you the things that really matter, not worthless junk of this world, and you will be transformed by His goodness and His grace.

Whew . . . what a blessing.

Jeremiah 17:7-8, "But blessed is the one who trusts in the Lord, whose confidence is in him. They will be like a tree planted by the water that sends out its roots by the stream. It does not fear when heat comes; its leaves are always green. It has no worries in a year of drought and never fails to bear fruit."

Face Time with God

My newest favorite thing is FaceTime. When I was little, I was fascinated with the Jetsons and how they could see each other on a screen when they talked. Well, the future is here and I love it. Earlier this week my daughter and I used FaceTime to connect from South Carolina to Texas and what a joy it was! My granddaughter squealed with delight when she saw my face and I squealed appropriately in response. It's not as good as being there in person, but it sure is closer than just hearing their voices. I was able to enjoy the smiles and almost feel like I was sitting there on the bed with them, laughing, talking and just loving each other. This got me to thinking about mature relationships.

When I was a little girl, I loved my daddy. Once a year, he and my mom would go on a company trip and I would stay with my Grandmother Johns. I was always excited for them to return, simply because I loved them but also because they always returned with "stuff." This stuff was the little trinkets from their trip for my sisters and me. We would hug them first and then ask, "What did you bring me?" It's not that we didn't love them simply for returning; we were just young and immature. Somehow we always expected something more than just their presence.

Today, it's different. I am more mature --- thank goodness --- and I adore my daddy just for being who he is. He is my father and my friend . . . one who loves me unconditionally. We have no expectations for each other except that we love each other. We don't need gifts or trinkets anymore. We just need each other. I want to hear his voice and see his face and enjoy being his daughter and this is what our relationship should be with God as well.

Too often we look to God only as Provider. "God, I need this, and I need that. God, I need you to meet this need and answer this prayer." Are those bad things? No, absolutely not. God tells us to cast our cares on Him because He cares for us. But that should never be the priority of our relationship with God. The most important part of our connection with God, the Father, is to seek His face, to desire simply to be in His presence and be loved by Him. We need to squeal with delight every time we sense His presence and we need to hunger for time with Him, simply because of *who* He is --- *not* what He can do for us. We need to call on His name every morning to start our day, talking with our Creator and our Savior. We need to call on His name continuously throughout the day, living with an attitude of thankfulness for Him and His love. We need to call on His name in the evening as we prepare to rest, trusting that He is with us in the darkest night, just as my earthly father used to watch over me after I went to sleep. God wants to meet our every need, but first we must delight in Him. Delight, what a wonderful word to characterize our connection to God...pure, honest delight.

So today I encourage you to approach God as Father. Ask Him for some FaceTime just because you want to sense His Presence and feel the love of the one who loves you and me unconditionally. Spend time at the foot of the Cross where Jesus gave His life for us out of total love and sacrifice; thank Him for that incredible gift. Talk to Him, love Him, and know Him more intimately with each conversation, and the more you know Him, the more you will hunger for Him and seek His face. Then, take your requests to God, who is waiting to bless you because you are His child. FaceTime with the Father will put a smile on your face and peace in your heart and there is no greater thing than this: being a child of the King.

Jeremiah 29:12-13, "Then you will call upon me and come and pray to me, and I will listen to you. You will seek me and find me when you seek me with all your heart."

Blanket People

In my home, we are blanket people. Right now in my den there are at least six blankets, all sizes, descriptions and textures. They are folded and placed neatly on the backs of couches and chairs, but that won't last. Later today they will be used as a warm, cozy covering, shielding Dan and me from the ceiling fan's activity or placed on the floor for my youngest granddaughter. And there are more blankets in my house. My writing room has one; my playroom has one and my guest bedroom has a very special one, made by my grandmother. I have given my children blankets as birthday gifts and Christmas stocking stuffers and every time I see one in a store . . . a pretty one that seems to need a home . . . I am tempted to purchase just one more. You see, we are blanket people.

My daughter has been infected with this same wonderful disease. Her collection is not as big as mine, but she's getting there and when she gets a new one, she just has to tell me about it. Her favorite one has a beautiful fall pattern and it's like wrapping in a cocoon. Covered and comforted. That's the magic of throw blankets. They cover us, warm us and protect us from the elements. If they are too short, they are no good. If they are nappy; it's time to give them away. If they are not soft enough, they never make it home with me. Blankets provide a covering that protects us from the cold and the wind; they just make life feel better. And God does the very same thing for us, if we will let Him.

God promises in scripture that He will cover us with His wings. In fact, Psalm 91:4, puts it this way, "He will cover you with His feathers; you will take refuge under His wings. His faithfulness will be a protective shield." I have felt recently like I needed a protective shield in my life. How about you? Life has sent some disasters my way and I feel like I've been repairing my armor or dodging a bullet for the last few weeks. And yet, during all of this, I have felt covered --- covered by God's protective wings. Just as I take refuge from the cold under my favorite blanket, I have taken refuge from the world's harshness in the arms of God, my Father.

Recently I faced surgery and for some reason, I felt very uneasy heading toward the hospital. I had prayed; my friends and family were praying and yet, I still felt a sense of foreboding. Then I reached into my heart for scripture and God gave me a vision: I imagined Him sending two angels of protection for my bed --- one at the head and one at the foot. I knew they would be there with me the whole time, watching over me during the procedure and, at that moment, I found peace. And, it gets better. God also sent two precious Christian sisters to me that morning before surgery. They work at the hospital and they came by to make sure things were going as they should and to give me the comfort of their presence. Coincidence? No. God sent them as my "angels" to cover me that morning.

Do you need a covering today? Do you need to find a place of refuge, a protective shield against the storms of life raging around you? God is waiting to "cover you with His feathers" and let you know that you are never alone. He is always there, like the perfect parent, covering you with His blanket of love, mercy, and protection. Life will go on and bad things will happen, but His protective arms are always bigger than our earthly problems. Run to Him and let Him cover you today.

Chain Saw Power

I once heard a pastor tell the story of a man who went to the hardware store and bought a chain saw. He was quite excited because his friends had told him that it would make his work of cutting trees so much easier. He took that chain saw home and immediately set himself to work, but, in no time at all, he was frustrated. He didn't seem to be making any progress because the trees weren't falling. So, back to the store he went to complain about this ineffective tool. He took the chain saw into the store and told the owner that it simply didn't work. The owner asked to see the chain saw, pulled the starter cord, and listened to it run. The man was shocked! He told the owner, "I didn't know I had to pull that cord. I've just been sawing back and forth and nothing has been happening."

Stupid story? Maybe not . . . the man had power in his hands and he didn't even recognize it. Are we so different?

As Christians we are promised power and authority based on the name of Jesus, and yet most days we live without ever pulling the cord on the chain saw. We pray but not expectantly. We ask but not boldly. We beg but don't thank God for the answer before it comes. And sometimes we simply don't ask at all, fearful that God doesn't want to hear our petitions, but He does. In Mark 11:22-24, the Bible says, "'Have faith in God,' Jesus answered. 'I tell you the truth, if anyone says to this mountain, 'Go, throw yourself into the sea,' and does not doubt in his heart but believes what he says will happen, it will be done for him. Therefore, I tell you, whatever you ask for in prayer, believe that you have received it and it will be yours.'" These are powerful verbs of authority. Let's take a look at them for just a moment:

Have faith. We must have faith in God, not in ourselves and our human abilities but in God's ability to do the impossible. When we bring even a little faith to the Lord, we find that He is all-sufficient to meet our every need.

Not **doubt**. It's so easy to ask and then slip into doubt because we are human and we know *we* are unable to do the impossible, but God relishes in doing the impossible. We must trust him and not doubt; He will answer and then *He* will be glorified in our lives.

Believe. Look back over the course of your life. Remember the times God has answered you in the past. Let it be your reminder to believe Him again today, no matter the gravity of your current situation.

Ask in prayer. Don't call your friend and ask. Don't call your boss and ask. Ask *God* in prayer for your deepest needs and your simplest concerns. He loves us and is waiting to bless us. We simply must ask.

When I was growing up in the church, we often sang "There's Power in the Blood," and until a few years ago, I never really gave that song much thought. But the truth is this: there *is* power in the blood --- the blood of Jesus. The blood that He shed on the Cross has the power to save us from our sinfulness. The blood that He shed on the Cross has the power to redeem all mankind. The blood of Jesus takes sinful, hopeless people and washes us whiter as snow. That same power is available to us today in our lives, and yet we often fail to pray with the authority of the blood. Do you want power in your life? Pray the blood of Jesus over every situation that would discourage and defeat you. Satan has no power against the blood of Jesus and with that prayer the mountain of defeat that he throws at us will be tossed into the sea. I like to think it drowns in the depths of the Atlantic, never to be seen again.

In the New Testament, Jesus gave a bunch of fishermen the authority and power to heal and preach in His name. They weren't any more special than you and me, and they had no more gifts than we do. What they had, we have as well: the authority of Jesus Christ, our Savior.

Today, don't pray wimpy prayers. Pray boldly, knowing that God is waiting to hear you and meet you where you are. Pray with authority, asking Him to hold to His promises to protect us with His wings. Pull the cord on your chain saw so that trees of doubt fall before you and you live a life of power in Christ.

Hebrews 10: 19-22, "Therefore, brothers, since we have confidence to enter the Most Holy Place by the blood of Jesus, by a new and living way opened for us through the curtain, that is, his body, and since we have a great priest over the house of God, let us draw near to God with a sincere heart in full assurance of faith, having our hearts sprinkled to cleanse us from a guilty conscience and having our bodies washed with pure water."

1 John 5: 14-15, "This is the confidence we have in approaching God: that if we ask anything according to his will, he hears us. And if we know that he hears us—whatever we ask—we know that we have what we asked of him."

Ephesians 3: 20-21, "Now to him who is able to do immeasurably more than all we can ask or imagine, according to his power that is at work within us, to him be glory in the church and in Christ Jesus throughout all generations, for ever and ever, Amen!"

Connecting the Dots of Ministry

Last night I had the privilege of witnessing to a young gay man who struggles with meth addiction. Last weekend, I received a beautiful, heart-felt letter and picture from a prison inmate who committed murder. He calls us collect on a weekly basis and he speaks to me as Aunt Jean, even though we are not related by blood or culture. A few months ago, a young man from Columbia stayed in our home; he had recently been released from prison and we stay connected by phone.

Unusual connections? Yes. Unwanted? No, not at all

I would love to tell you the whole story of how our lives have become intertwined and maybe one day I will, but for now, that piece is private out of respect for stories that only others will tell. But here's what God spoke into my heart in the darkness of my parlor this morning: ministry doesn't always happen in the pristine doors of our churches. Ministry is messy and costly and sometimes tiring, but in every case, if God has blessed us with a place of ministry that takes our breath away, we must thank Him for connecting the dots of our lives with those who need us most.

Jesus didn't spend his three years of ministry with people who were well; He sought people who needed him. He reached out to the sick, the lost, and the hungry. He spoke with crowds who were desperate to hear the words of a Savior. He loved the unlovable. He served those who needed Him most.

This morning I thanked God for giving me Jesus as my model of how to behave in a world of hopelessness and despair. The model is one of love and inclusion.

I teach middle school and I love every single student I teach. I love the ones who come from homes where life is safe and meals are a sure thing. But I also love the ones who show up needing a hug, a breakfast, and the assurance that someone in life is stable and consistent --- the ones who needs to be assured every day that someone loves them and lights up when they enter the classroom door. I serve them all, but I live to serve the ones who need me most.

We all are called to do God's work . . . *His* work – not ours. We should never serve on a committee or sing in a choir at church if it is not God's will for our lives because here's what happens. We get "busy" for the Lord and then we are never quiet and still enough to listen for the messy, difficult ministry to which He is calling us. We get tired with serving and just maybe we're doing things God never intended. Ministry should invigorate us because we are being His hands and feet to the world. Now don't misquote me: there are crucial areas of ministry that don't involve the hard roads of life. I think immediately of Sunday School teachers who have allowed God to use them to teach and transform others. I think of nursery workers who allow young mothers and fathers to worship together in God's house. I think of the prayer warriors who spend their lives interceding on behalf of all of us. This is not quite as messy, but is critically important to the Kingdom.

So here's the essential question: what is God calling you to do today? Is He asking you to continue where you are in your place of service? Then continue. Is He closing a door so He can open another one? Then trust Him and leave that door shut. Is He asking you, like He has asked me in recent days, to do something that's a challenge but a privilege? If He is, say yes, and say it with abandon. You will be so blessed when you bless others, which brings me to Clayton.

Clayton is the man who wrote me the poetic letter last week. He calls me and we talk about life. He has some pretty amazing thoughts and lessons he can share . . . lessons learned from time spent in a small cell with lots of hours to do nothing but think. Clayton called last week to check on a family member... our connection. I was tired and was in the middle of a task that had to be completed, so I really didn't want to answer the phone that late afternoon, but I did. It was almost time to go to evening services at church, so my heart was in a rush, but Clayton was not. He needed to remind me of something urgent and his question could have been insulting, but you see, it wasn't. I knew his heart was in the right place. Clayton asked me how many times we have had "family conferences" with our relative.

Family conferences? Yes, he said. How often do you sit down with him, just to find out his insecurities and his needs?

Wow. Wow. Wow again.

I wanted to defend myself, but the truth is, I couldn't. Clayton reminded me that love must be intentional. Sometimes it needs to spring from a spontaneous moment, but at other times, it needs to be supported by a planned, intentional family meeting where we give 100% of our hearts and our attention to the one who needs it most. Clayton saw the deepest hurts of our family member and the lack of confidence that shows up in a cell with longs days and nights and nothing to do but talk. Clayton was a minister to the one who needed it most. It took time and listening ears and he gave both. We had the first of what I hope to be many family conferences this weekend; God was in it and the power of a family wrapped around a life made a world of difference --- a life-saving difference.

Who is the one who needs God's love most in your life? I can't answer that, but I can recommend this: slow down and let God connect the dots of your love for Him with those who need Him most. You will be blessed and God's kingdom will be glorified. Maybe the one you take time for today will be the one lost sheep who will find the fold and allow the guiding of the Great Shepherd to transform his life forever. Thanks be to God!

Matthew 25:40, "The King will reply, 'Truly I tell you, whatever you did for one of the least of these brothers and sisters of mine, you did for me.'"

Speak Blessings

I recently watched the movie *The Help*, after reading the book first, of course, and it was wonderful. One certain part of it stuck with me when it was over: Aibileen Clark's words to Mae Mobley, the little girl in her care. Over and over she spoke these words to Mae, having her repeat them after her: "You is kind. You is smart. You is important." These words were crucial to little Mae because her own mother failed to speak words of blessing over her. She failed to give her the time that mothers owe their children, and so as was often the case in that day and culture, the "help" had to step in and do what that mother didn't find time or energy to do. And it's the thing God does for us every single day.

If you are waiting on the world to tell you that you are kind, smart, and important, stop waiting. Stop expecting. Stop depending on a fractured world to give you what you need. It will fail you over and over because it is flawed and broken. It just is. I was blessed to grow up in a family that believed in me and spoke blessings over my life, so I naively believed that the world would do the same, and sometimes it does, but it's often short-lived or shallow. The only blessings with real depth and grace are those that come from God, and when He says, "You is kind. You is smart. You is important," you have received the blessings of the God of the universe. And He has the power to make us all of that and more, but He also expects us to pay it forward.

During this year, make a decision to do three things: 1) Read the Bible and find blessings for your life in the living, breathing Word of

God. They are waiting to leap off the pages into your heart; they are eternal and always true. 2) Talk to God daily. Start every prayer with thanksgiving for the blessings He has already given . . . even the hard times because God takes those and brings unexpected favor at the worst moments. Then ask Him to bless your life. Every day. 3) Finally, pay it forward. Be intentional about speaking words of blessing over the lives of those around you – your children, your family, your co-workers and the people you meet on the street. Let them feel the love of God through you; love them because God first loved you. He loves me and I know I don't deserve it, not a single day, but He loves me anyway and blesses my life. So, I want to do the same for others.

Be an Aibileen for someone today. Remember her simple but profound words to Mae: "You is kind. You is smart. You is important." See others and yourself with God's eyes, and let His blessings abound. It's not complicated. It's simply amazing grace.

John 13:34-35, "I give you a new command: Love one another. Just as I have loved you, you must also love one another. [35] By this all people will know that you are My disciples, if you have love for one another."

Living in Awe

I picked up my computer this morning, planning to write a devotional that's been on my mind about silver, but that plan changed in a hurry. As I opened iTunes on my computer to listen to Christian music, I immediately heard the words of a Stephen Curtis Chapman song, and they changed my focus and my plan. Isn't God like that? As soon as we think, in our limited understanding, that we know where we're headed and what we're doing, God says, "Wait just a minute . . . let me show you something else." And what must we do? Listen. Just listen, and then follow. The Chapman song's lyrics speak of standing in awe of God's creation and realizing that it's not about us; it's about Him.

In the last year, I have been blessed to hear pastors who have taught me to slow down and be in awe of God's creations. And I do mean *taught.* You would think that I would not have needed that lesson, but I did. I have always been a multi-tasker, even before the term became popular. I just called myself incredibly busy, and in the midst of that "busy-ness," I would notice beautiful things, but I never stopped to thank God for those stunning scenes. I saw the beauty but failed to give God the credit. Now I have learned that these moments of amazement are opportunities to thank God for His creative work, to praise God for creating elements of nature that take my breath away, to stand in wonder of the Atlantic Ocean and know that He made that vast and powerful panorama. But there's another lesson, and it's in Chapman's lyrics.

How can I think this is all about me? We tend to be such egocentric personalities, constantly (and erroneously) thinking that somehow the world revolves around us. News flash: it doesn't. God loves us and desperately wants a relationship with us, but at the end of the day, it's not about us; it's about *Him*. It's about worshiping Him, giving Him glory, praising His name, loving Him, and being awed by His power, goodness, and mercy. So this morning, I want to make much of Jesus Christ, my Savior, and I want to remind others to do the same. I want to give Him my life . . . the total package . . . and thank Him that it can be used to make much of Him, to glorify Him, to honor Him.

I don't know where you are in your relationship with the Creator of the universe. Maybe you already live in wonder and awe of all that came from God's hand. Or maybe, like me, you needed this lesson. Wherever you are, remember today that it's about God. Use your day, your time, your thoughts, and your energy to make much of Him. And I promise you this: when you take the focus off yourself . . . just a sinner . . . and place it where it belongs . . . on the Savior . . . you will be blessed in ways that will leave you speechless.

Psalm 19:1, "The heavens declare the glory of God, and the sky proclaims the work of His hands."

God Gives Us What We Need

I've heard of Murphy's Law all my life, but in the last two weeks, I've been living it. Anybody else ever have that experience? My AC quit in my car, the lines to my bathtubs had to be replaced and my husband, Dan's, truck had to be repaired. But there's more. Our farm was robbed, a family member has been in major personal crisis and I found out that I have to undergo surgery. But there's more. My washing machine hasn't worked in two weeks and because we couldn't find our receipt, we are waiting on Lowe's to send a copy so we can use the warranty. Copies take ten ---yes, ten --- days. Are you kidding me? So I've found a great Laundromat for the moments when I'm out of underwear and bath towels. (☺) But the final straw was this morning. I woke up to make my coffee and the pot wouldn't perk. Just like that!

Perfect yesterday, broken today, isn't life like that? Perfect one moment and a complete mess the next!

Thank God, we are not alone. God is the master of helping us deal with the messes of life – both the ones we create and ones that surprise us like a 2X4 in the back of the head. And, because I have felt like the messes were getting the best of me, I did what I *know* to do: I have spent the last three days seeking God first thing in the morning. Not in the afternoon; not at night when I'm exhausted, but with my first cup of coffee. There's a cat in my lap, a dog by my side and God's name on my lips. It's where I find everything I need to triumph over the disasters of living life in a messed up world. This morning during my prayer time, I received a powerful but simple revelation from Him: He is exactly *what* we need *when* we need it. I needed a **friend** with whom I could confide; Jesus is my friend; He let me talk and reminded me to listen, too. I needed a **Father** who would let me sit at His feet and be comforted; He is the Great Comforter. I needed **power** to overcome foreboding thinking this morning and He is all powerful. The power of the blood of Jesus is all we need and I asked for a full measure this morning. I needed an **advisor** and God is surely the best because His Word tells us that He has a plan laid out for our lives. We just need to ask for the Holy Spirit to guide us toward that perfect plan that is already prepared. Finally, I needed **love**. I needed unconditional love, a love so great that it washes over me and cleanses my spirit. God is love. He doesn't *just* love us. He *IS* love. And I think that's where my mind and spirit are going to camp today. I need to know that when I disappoint Him (which is way too often) He loves me. I need to know that when I feel like I'm drowning in the Murphy's Law moments of life, He loves me. I need to know that I can give up trying to control things that are beyond my "pay grade" because He will handle those things. He does it because He is God. His plan is perfect. And He loves me.

He loves you in that very same way. Sadly, not everyone believes that. This week as I talked with a family member in crisis, I told him to seek a particular church in his area where I knew he could receive love and support. He responded almost angrily, "There's no church that will help me." I also told him that he desperately needs to ask God to help, and I promised to pray for him. He scoffed at that, and rebuffed my attempts to be a prayer support. See, he doesn't get it that God loves him . . . purely, unconditionally, and completely. No matter what he has done or where he has been or how many times he has fallen into sin --- God loves him. If we could all get that deep in our spirits, it would change so many things. Our trust in His complete love for us would help us to love others in that same way. After all, don't we want others to have the love we feel...to share in the joy of being God's children?

So, in the coming days, I'm going to do a few things and I invite you to join me. First, I'm going to focus on the simplicity and beauty of God's love for me. Every day, all day. He loves me and He loves you, too. Second, I'm going to pay more attention to the things around me that He's already doing and I'm going to find ways to share His love through the gifts and talents He has allowed me to have. Finally, I'm going to continue to give Him the first part of my day. When I start the day talking to my Father, my dearest Friend, my Comforter and my Redeemer, the Murphy's Law moments will simply be a blip on the screen but my eyes will be on Jesus. What a beautiful sight!

Hebrews 12: 1-2, "Therefore, since we also have such a large cloud of witnesses surrounding us, let us lay aside every weight and the sin that so easily ensnares us. Let us run with endurance the race that lies before us, ² keeping our eyes on Jesus,[a] the source and perfecter[b] of our faith, who for the joy that lay before Him[c] endured a cross and despised the shame and has sat down at the right hand of God's throne."

Quality . . . Not Quantity

"How long does it have to be?" It was the only question in my middle school ELA classroom that aggravated my heart (and made me want to say, "Seriously?") It reveals a very telling fact: the students who ask this haven't really begun to see themselves as writers. They haven't begun to understand that writing is about telling your story, creating a piece that compels readers to read, drawing images with which others can connect. It's not about length. I often answer, "What do you need to say? Have you said it well? Have you conveyed your story? Then it's long enough." They don't understand right away, but as I help them develop themselves as writers, the writers' light bulb comes on for many of them and they never ask the question again. They become free to *be* writers, not followers of a prescribed plan. They learn to work for quality, not quantity. As Christians, we could do well to learn that lesson, too.

I'm going to admit something terrible, but maybe some of you will understand: I spent years going to church without spending time studying God's word. I attended every choir practice, every activity and every Sunday School class, but I didn't study at home. I didn't dig through my Bible, meditating on scripture. Well, now I do. Now I have a hunger for God's Word . . . still not enough sometimes, but a hunger, nonetheless and yes . . . my quantity of study has increased, but it's the quality of my study that really matters. I don't compare myself to others who study more and I don't time myself or set crazy goals I can't reach. It's about the quality and God knows that I am continually striving to be a better student of His word. I believe He is pleased with that, but it's not the only place where quality counts.

I wish I could tell you that I spend hours every day on my knees, praying and listening to God, but I can't. I pray every day . . . sometimes much longer than others and sometimes just words scattered throughout the day. I'm not Mother Teresa and I've not arrived at a magic number, but I do talk to God, my Father, every day. Sometimes I talk to Him while I'm driving, other times I talk to Him through the words of songs that speak for me. Sometimes I sit on a cool bench under an old oak and find Him there, and other times, I cry out from the "mom" space in my house. I have prayed face down on the floor, on my knees, and holding my head in my hands, but the point is this: I have learned to pray with honesty without flowery words . . . just honesty. I always begin with praise and thanksgiving and sometimes it ends there, but other times, I spend time interceding for myself and for those I know, those I love, and those whose names have been sent to me in prayer. I pray for direction and guidance, thanking God that He loves me, that He hears me and that He has a plan for my life. And the truth is? It's not always long, but it's the quality of my heart that counts.

Years ago, a friend and supervisor told me that I couldn't be a writing teacher without being a writer. "Phooey," I said. (Well, that's not exactly what I said, but you get the idea.) I can give them the rules, the formulas, and the lessons. I don't have time to write. I'm a busy mom, teacher, church-goer and wife, and I really don't have time to do my own writing.

"But you have to journal," she said. "Yeah, right," I answered. "Would that be before the laundry or after I grade 300 papers tonight?" Well, the irony of all ironies: I went to a Joyce Meyer conference a few years ago and she said this: "You need to write scriptures down in long hand." I believed. I bought my first journal and that was many journals ago. Since then, I've learned to write more than just scriptures and God has allowed me to write for Him. But before you think my writing is rambling off topic, let me make the point: just like I can't be the best writing teacher without being a writer, I can't be the witness God wants me to be without living in His Word and talking to Him daily. I can know the rules and the formulas, but until I walk it out with Him in my daily life, it won't really work in the world or in my heart. Now, don't get me wrong. It's not about following certain rules for journaling or praying or even studying: it's about giving God the *best* time that I can give Him, whether it's fifteen minutes or five hours, because it's all about quality, not quantity. And when I give Him my heart, He honors it every time.

Now, I do want to contradict myself just for a moment. Today, and in the past days, He has reminded me that for right now, quantity *is* a little more important than usual. I've just had surgery and I need to rest. He has reminded me daily that it's rare for me to have this much time to devote to Him, and I should use it wisely. It's easy to let Satan convince me that I just have to see one more daytime TV show or one more rerun of *Criminal Minds*, but I don't. That's Satan, trying his best to make me waste these precious days and hours in which I have absolutely nothing to do but recover in body and spirit. When I return to work or am able to cook and clean again (Gee, could I just leave those off forever?), things will change, and I'll be back to rushed days and way too much to do; then the quality of my time with Him will outweigh the quantity once again, but until then? I'm going to live in His presence, and make the most of every single moment He is using to do what He does so well: "He makes me lie down in green pastures; He leads me beside still waters; He restores my soul." Wow . . . sounds like an offer I can't refuse.

2 Timothy 2:15, "Do your best to present yourself to God as one approved, a worker who has no need to be ashamed, rightly handling the word of truth."

Psalm 5:3, "In the morning, LORD, you hear my voice; in the morning I lay my requests before you and wait expectantly."

One-to-One Savior

I am a school teacher, and in year 34, I will again be learning new and innovative ways to reach children. In my school, we will be doing one-to-one computing next year. Every single sixth grader will have a Mac Air, and we will be utilizing blended learning – a true blend of best teaching practices and best technical learning and support. Why is this such a big deal? In this world of so many needs in our children, we are finding a way to reach every single child where he or she is. We are giving them one-on-one instruction as well as small group lessons and intervention. Every child's needs will be met --- that's the big goal, and we believe, as others do, that this will change the way middle schools do business for children. But long before computers enabled us to reach students one-to-one, Jesus reached out to individuals . . . one-to-one.

In many Bible stories, we hear of Jesus speaking to the multitudes. He taught to the crowds of thousands, and He spent time with His group of disciples. But Jesus also loved and responded to individuals with personal, private encounters - - -one-to-one. We see a beautiful example in John 4: the story of the woman at the well. Jesus was passing through Samaria when He encountered a Samaritan woman who had come to the well in the middle of the day to draw water. She was there with two purposes: the obvious is that she needed water. The less obvious is that she came in the middle of the day to avoid other people. She was not respected in the community because she had a less than stellar past and a present that was no better. Can anybody relate? I sure can. Anyway, she was a mess, a broken spirit in need of a one-to-one encounter with a Holy God, and Jesus provided just that. He spoke to her, offering her more than just the physical water she was seeking. He revealed Himself to her as the Messiah she anticipated. She had a one-to-one encounter with truth, respect, and a Savior who could heal her wounded soul. He was just what she needed, and God offers that to each and every one of us every single day.

I love corporate worship. I love singing and praising God; I love sitting in His presence in a sanctuary; I love learning His Word in Bible study classes and through a powerful sermon. But that's not near enough. I need --- *we* need --- a one-on-one relationship with our Savior. We need to meet Him at the well of our lives and drink deeply from His living water. We need to speak to Him privately, honestly and humbly, bowing before Him and seeking His forgiveness, His guidance, and most importantly, His face. We were created with a need for God, and a personal relationship with Him is the only peg that will fill that mighty hole in our spirits. It can't be done with religion . . . only with a one-on-one, ongoing connectedness to God, our Father.

And so, we must listen intentionally and turn our hearts to God. Jesus calls out to us in the tumult of life in a society that is screaming everything *but* the name of a Savior. Jesus calls out to us in the quietness of our personal desperation. Jesus calls out to us, saying, "I love you so much that I went to the Cross just for you . . . *just for you.*" Will you answer Him today and share some one-on-one time with the only one who can forgive your past, strengthen your present, and transform your future? He Is the God who Was, and Is, and Is to Come. He is waiting on your private response. Allow yourself to be compelled, as was the woman with the alabaster box...to seek Him above all else and to be oblivious to everything else. It's just about you and Him: one-on-one.

Running to Jesus

I was eating lunch with a friend at work a few days ago, and she was telling a story that, sadly enough, happens way too often. She was driving through town and drove up on a chaotic situation; there had been a drive-by shooting, and people --- children included --- were running to see what had happened. She shared how upset this made her and that she let loose a diatribe, telling the children to go home, that being nosy during a tragedy is wrong. I don't think they listened. And this is not the only kind of situation that people clamor to see.

Every morning when I open my computer, I see stories that I don't even want or need to know . . . stories of actors' ugly divorces, stories of unfaithful Congressmen, stories of famous people in rehab . . . I choose not to read them. And yet, they are printed daily and chased by "journalists" (I use that term lightly) because the public, as a whole, is incredibly fascinated with the lives of the rich and famous. We also seem to have a new fascination with the lives of people who, before the age of reality TV, never would have crossed our minds. We live in a "Honey Boo-Boo" age. We run to see these people, some whose lives, quite honestly, are offensive and/or embarrassing, and yet we run to them. But I would suggest that we are running in all the wrong paths.

This morning, as I was reading scripture, I came across this verse: "But the man went and spread the word, proclaiming to everyone what had happened. As a result, large crowds soon surrounded Jesus, and he couldn't publicly enter a town anywhere. He had to stay out in the secluded places, but people from everywhere kept coming to him." (Mark 1:45) This verse follows a narrative of many of the miracles that Jesus performed, and because people learned of His power, they were running to him. We read other stories of people running to him, too: children who gathered at his knees, a woman with years of bleeding who fought through a crowd just to touch the hem of His garment, a family who ran to Him because Lazarus was sick and dying. People heard, and people ran to Him. Why? Because He had the power to heal and change lives, and He still has that power today, and yet too many people are so busy running to the wrong things that they are not running to Jesus.

In the past six months, I have had some serious health problems. After trying to solve them myself and spending some pretty miserable days, I finally saw my family physician and then a specialist, but before I saw the rheumatologist, I did the most important thing: I visited a friend at school and shared my pain. She held my hands and prayed over me . . . a powerful prayer of healing, thanking God that the healing was already complete. I continued to hurt, and yet I also continued to believe that healing was coming. I still kept my appointment with the doctor, who gave me some shots and some advice. I listened and obeyed, and during the Christmas break, my pain stopped. Completely. I'm not even taking the medicine he recommended. Did the shots probably help? Sure. Did the new shoes the doctor made me buy make a difference? Sure. Did God send me the healing I so desperately needed? Absolutely. He used that doctor to provide wise counsel, and yet I am very sure He did the rest because *I believed* He would. People say miracles don't happen today, but they are wrong. I am pain-free this morning, and I know God is the Great Healer. And I am running to Him . . . every day, in every way.

One of my favorite songs says that we are to run with abandon to the Mercy Seat of Christ; He sits there, waiting to comfort and provide healing for our souls. Every day, Jesus is still waiting at the Mercy Seat --- waiting for you and me...waiting for us to come running to Him. Waiting for us to put Him above all else. Waiting for us to repent of running to other things and instead, run first and only to Him. He is waiting to provide grace and forgiveness and healing, but first we must come running. *Not* to the world, *not* to the phone, *not* to the latest news story, but *to Him*, the only Savior who can transform your life and heal your heart. He is waiting and calling out to you. Are you ready to run to Him?

Hebrews 4: 16, "Therefore let us approach the throne of grace with boldness, so that we may receive mercy and find grace to help us at the proper time."

It's Not About Us

"God does not exist to make a big deal out of us. We exist to make a big deal out of him. It's not about you. It's not about me. It's all about Him." [1] --Max Lucado

We live in a world today that would convince us that everything is all about us. Mirrors everywhere, infomercials for weight loss, people who tell us we "deserve" certain things. It's a mirage . . . a very false and dangerous mirage, and it is teaching our young people a scary untruth: the world revolves around you and only you, and you need to grab everything you want, even if it requires hurting others or yourself. Well, this week I was joyfully surprised to hear just the opposite.

I asked my new 7th grade students to work in groups to decide what our classroom rules *really* mean. In one group, they were expected to tell the class what "be thoughtful and respectful" looks and sounds like in our classroom environment. The first thing one young man said was this: "It means you have to always think about how your words and actions are going to affect the people around you." The wisdom of a 7th grader; it's days like this that keep me in the classroom. And he's right. Too many people only consider how decisions and words affect themselves, never reaching beyond their own personal space to ponder the needs and hearts of others. Just look at some of the things people post on Facebook to prove my point. I am going to enjoy my time with this student, but there's so much more.

There's a Stephen Curtis Chapman song in which he says that we must make much of Jesus and the Cross; Chapman got it right: God created us to worship Him, to praise Him, and to make much of Him. He didn't create us to be self-centered, living our lives with no thought of Him. We *are* His. He is our Father, and we are to worship Him. And yet, so many people come to the corporate worship experience unprepared to truly worship Him. I have been guilty myself so many times. We sleep late on Sunday morning, rush to get dressed, and spend more time preparing our "look" than our hearts. We put off praying until we get to church, instead of praying in preparation for being with other believers in God's presence. We enter the service at the last moment, chatting with our friends instead of silencing our hearts for worship. And then? We sing, but it doesn't even begin to have a glimmer of the enthusiasm and excitement we had last night while watching our favorite football team. Now don't misunderstand me: every person worships differently, and you don't have to lift your hands and sing loudly to show your love for God, but our faces should surely be transformed during worship. We cannot possibly have an authentic encounter with Holy God without allowing Him to reach into our hearts during worship, drawing us unto Him. Sometimes for me it means "lifting my hands in the sanctuary" as the Psalmist says, and sometimes it means I can't mouth the words at all: I just close my eyes and stand in silent awe. But the point is this: it's all about Him. It's not about us. It's not about going to church to be fed. We were not created to be coddled by a pastor or a service; we were created to worship Almighty God. And when we do that, He makes a big deal out of us. He blesses us and transforms us from the inside out. He puts His glasses on us so we see Him and others differently --- *like He sees.*

Today I pray that you are drawn by God to worship Him with abandon. I pray that you are compelled by God to spend time in His presence --- just because you want to make much of Him. I pray that you are awed to realize that it's not about you . . . it's about Him, our Lord and Master. Thank goodness: for so long I thought it was all about me. Sure does take the pressure off.

Revelation 4:11, "You are worthy, our Lord and God, to receive glory and honor and power, for you created all things, and by your will they were created and have their being."

Nehemiah 9:6, "You alone are the LORD. You made the heavens, even the highest heavens, and all their starry host, the earth and all that is on it, the seas and all that is in them. You give life to everything, and the multitudes of heaven worship you.

[1] From Max Lucado, *The Lucado Inspirational Reader*, page 443

Healthy Soil

My sweet husband, Dan, loves to grow a garden, and I love to eat, so we're a great match. A number of years ago, I bought him a tiller at an auction, and from that day, he became a gardener extraordinaire! He grows hot peppers, cabbage, bell peppers and cucumbers . . . lots of great green stuff that my body loves and appreciates. So this year, it was not a surprise that when we bought a piece of farm property, he started a garden down there. During the summer it went reasonably well and so, this fall, he planted sweet potatoes. Here's where the story takes a sad farmer's turn.

A couple of weeks ago, he decided to dig the sweet potatoes, and I was so excited. I gathered my bucket and watched with great anticipation as the shovel opened the ground, looking for the precious orange treasures. But what came out was so funny that it was laughable: the sweet potatoes never grew past about two inches long. He found them, but they were the tiniest things I have ever seen. I asked him what happened, and he said that the farm soil just wasn't right for growth. He should have added lime . . . but he hadn't.

Soil without the right nutrients doesn't grow robust vegetables.

And so it is with our lives: without the right fertilizer and nutrients in place, we never grow to be all God desires for us.

In Matthew 13, we find Jesus' parable of the sower. He shared this from a boat because the crowds were so large, anxious to hear what He had to say. The parable says this:

"Then He told them many things in parables, saying: 'Consider the sower who went out to sow. As he was sowing, some seed fell along the path, and the birds came and ate them up. Others fell on rocky ground, where there wasn't much soil, and they sprang up quickly since the soil wasn't deep. But when the sun came up they

were scorched, and since they had no root, they withered. Others fell among thorns, and the thorns came up and choked them. Still others fell on good ground and produced a crop: some 100, some 60, and some 30 times what was sown. Anyone who has ears should listen.'" (Matthew 13: 3-9, HCSB)

Good soil. Even Jesus talked about it. So let's get straight to the heart of the matter: what kind of ground are you? Has the Word been shared with you, but because your heart is rocky, it never even had a chance to take root and change your life? Or is your heart so full of thorns that even God's Word is choked out? Choked out by the weeds that look good in the world but destroy what God desires for us? Or are you creating good soil for God's Word?

Good soil . . . soil with all the nutrients needed for healthy growth. Are you adding the lime you need to prepare yourself to hear and hide God's Word in your heart?

It's time to prepare, and so today I am calling you to action, whatever it is you need.

Action #1: Communicate with God. Talk to Him as your Father, your Friend, your Comforter, and your Strength. Talk to Jesus as Savior and Redeemer. Open your heart simply by calling on His name and allowing Him to speak words into your life. It doesn't require a fancy, impressive prayer; it just requires calling out to Him; He has promised to listen.

Action #2: Read His Word. His Word is the seed, but if you never work on planting it in your heart you will never grow anything at all. And if you don't know where to start, find a simple, manageable devotional book, or go to youversion.com and pick a plan. Or, open the Bible and just begin. Maybe you want to start with the Old Testament so you understand the need for a Savior. Maybe you want to read the Gospels – Matthew, Mark, Luke and John --- so you hear the story and the voice of Jesus. Perhaps you might start with Psalms because you need to hear David singing and dancing with God, even in his despair and sin. Or possibly you need to start with Proverbs or James, great instructional books on how to live. Wherever you start, take it slowly and allow His Word to sink deeply into your heart.

My young adult Sunday School class is taking a different approach: every Sunday each person considers a need in his/her life . . . a need to forgive or not fear, etc. Then we find a scripture that addresses that exact need. They write scriptures on index cards, and we add one each week to a flip book we have created. The rings holding the flip books are big enough to go on the gear shift in our cars or on our key rings. They go with us wherever we go so we can remember and meditate on that verse all week. By the end of 2014, we will have searched for 52 meaningful scriptures to armor ourselves against the world and Satan's power.

Action #3: Ask Him to help you understand His Word. He has promised in scripture that we can ask for wisdom and He will provide.

Action #4: Know the schedule of opportunities for worship at your church and GO! I hear people say all the time that they don't need to go to church because it's not necessary and it's full of hypocrites. Wrong and wrong! It is most certainly necessary; Paul said that we should not fail to meet with other believers, that we might grow stronger together, serve together, and hold each other accountable. We can't do that alone. And, the church is not full of hypocrites; it's full of people who fall and are saved by God's grace, but so is the rest of the world. We are *all* sinners, saved by grace, and even in the church, people sin every day. It is the reality of our fallen condition. This is why we so desperately need grace: Satan will attack, and he usually focuses his efforts on destroying those who are living openly for Christ because he needs to ruin our witness in the world. And this, again, is why we need the church. We need to learn, grow, and support each other so he doesn't win . . . ever!

These are just a handful of ideas, but they are urgent ones. If you want to prepare your soil to hear God's Word, His plans for you, and His loving correction, you must prepare the soil of your heart and life. If you don't take time to add the "lime" you need, you will grow about as much as those puny sweet potatoes. And I know you want more. I surely do.

Momma's Table – Part II

Until a few years ago, I didn't have a table big enough to seat my entire family, but one day, our son, Asher, showed up with an incredible gift: a table large enough to fill a room and thrill my heart. There was only one problem: the table had no legs. He ended up with the table because the woman who ordered it found the top to be defective, and she chose to keep the legs but order another table top. So Asher, knowing how much I love family dinners, gave the top to Dan and me as a gift . . . with no legs. Of course, my ingenious husband figured out a way to eat on that table with make shift legs that year, but eventually, that free table had to have proper legs, and so we spent quite a bit to make that happen. In other words, the free gift turned out not to be so free. I love my table, and I cherish the family times we share there, but I also cherish the message God has given me through this amazing gift.

Just like that table, God's gift of grace is free to every single one of us, but there's more to know: the gift is free, but it will cost us to be able to enjoy this free gift.

Just like we had to purchase legs to make the table functional, as believers, we must spend to make our salvation glorify God and His Kingdom. Spend, you say? Yes. We must spend time --- time with God, time with others who need us most, time with the lost in order to share the love of God, time in worship, time in prayer, and time in study. Salvation is indeed free, but without spending time in the way God desires, we will never truly know Him, and we will not reach others in the way Jesus commanded. This free gift costs us time . . . and every minute spent is worth it.

This free gift also costs us energy. Living for God in response to His grace requires that we do things for Him, things to further His Kingdom. We have to get off our couches and the comfortable places of life and use our energy to go where He leads us. It's not always easy or convenient, but the energy used for God is well spent. We may be tired at the end of the day, but it's a good kind of tired, and He will give us rest.

This free gift also costs us because we have to give up things that we like to hold on to . . . things like unforgiveness, bitterness, anger, and a "why me" spirit. God asks us to give up those worthless feelings that never produce good fruit and exchange them for His love, His joy and His peace. It's a great exchange, but it means we have to spend our hearts in trusting God completely and knowing that His plan for us is always good.

And there's another lesson of the table that the Holy Spirit spoke into my heart this morning. Last weekend, we had Christmas dinner at the big table with our grandchildren, and there were empty seats. Empty because my precious Meredith, Jamie and Olivia didn't get to come home from Texas. There were empty seats because our son didn't get home in time to join us; empty seats because our darling Addelyn contracted the flu, keeping her and her mom away from us; empty seats because one chose not to participate.

Empty seats at the table

And there are tons of empty seats at God's table, too. There are so many in this world who do not call Him Lord . . . who do not know Him as the only baby who chose to come in order for us to be saved . . who do not know God as Father. They haven't joined His table, for whatever reason, and the seats are empty. And as long as even one seat is empty, God is calling out to all people to join His table of grace, blessings, forgiveness, peace and joy. He will not be satisfied as long as one person is lost, leaving a seat at the table without the child whose name He has engraved on that chair. Empty seats.

So we have some things to do. We need to do as Jesus commanded: "Go into all the world," telling people of His saving grace. We need to wear our "Jesus glasses" and see others the way God sees them, meeting their needs in His name. We need to look beyond ourselves and know that everything we do and say must honor His name and glorify His Kingdom. These are big tasks, but tasks worthy of our time, energy, and trust. And when our lives glorify the King, I believe the seats at His table of grace will be filled, and we will be blessed beyond measure.

John 15: 16-17, "You did not choose me, but I chose you and appointed you to go and bear fruit---fruit that will last. Then the Father will give you whatever you ask in my name. This is my commandment: Love each other."

Peddling Hope

My husband and I are crime drama junkies. We love *Criminal Minds, Blue Bloods,* and *Law & Order.*   And back in the day when one of our favorite characters, Lenny, was on *Law and Order*, we anxiously anticipated his cryptic puns and profound comments. We knew it was coming, and he never disappointed. Recently I was watching a marathon of shows and heard this quote from Lenny: "He's peddling hope, and there's nothing more addictive."   Another great Lenny moment, and there's a whole lot of truth in that statement.

Stop and think about all of the things in the world that "peddle hope," keeping us attached to them, whether negative or positive. Drugs . . . hope for the next high. Diets . . . hope for weight loss. Exercise . . . hope for a better body. Plastic surgery . . . hope for an immortal face. Facebook . . . hope for friends. Candy Crush . . . hope for victory. Heavy alcohol use . . . hope for dulling the pain.

Peddling hope. In the words of Lenny, it's addictive. I don't know anyone who doesn't hope for a better day, a better year, and a better life. And hope is a positive force when attached to positive, healthy thinking, but here's what I've learned in my life:

 Anything I hope for is just thoughts and wishes without the power of God to turn my hopes into reality.

Example . . . I have battled my weight going up and down since I was 19 years old. I've tried things I don't want to admit, and I've had success many times, but because I try to do the food thing in my own strength, I always slip. And I slip badly. I get my "head" right for a while, but then I get tired of denying myself the things I love, so I go back to decadent desserts, crisply fried French fries, and dark chocolate candy. Actually, any kind of candy.   And the result goes without saying.

So what must I --- and you --- do differently to have lasting hope and change? Plug into God's power concerning everything in our lives.

God doesn't peddle hope; He *is* hope.

When Mary and Martha had lost hope, Jesus raised their brother from the dead. When the woman with bleeding touched the hem of Jesus' garment, she was healed because she placed her hope and faith in Him. When the disciples didn't understand that Jesus really would be resurrected, He rose again, bringing hope to His followers. And the list goes on and on --- examples of people whose lives were changed because they found their hope in God. Lepers who were healed, hungry people who were fed with five loaves and two fishes, Israelites who ate manna that came down from heaven, and Wise Men who followed a star and found a King.

Hope came in the form of a baby, and He changed the world.

I heard Pastor Charles Nieman speak on television last week, and he gave this definition of the word *resurrection:* stand up and recovery. Jesus was resurrected: He stood up and recovered. The lame man was healed by Jesus, and He stood up and recovered. Over and over in my own life, I have asked for God's help and healing, and He has enabled me to stand up and recover from life's difficulties and heartaches. Stand up and recover. Sounds a lot like hope to me.

So how do we live with this kind of hope? We stay plugged in to the power plant: God. We connect to His power through prayer and studying His Word. We stay connected with Him all day, every day, praying without ceasing. We ask for His strength and His transforming power to be at work in our lives because, in the words of Rick Warren, "With God, today's impossibility is tomorrow's miracle." (from *The Daniel Plan* by Rick Warren)

I love the song "Everlasting God," and the first line says that we get stronger when we wait on God. I implore you to wait upon the Lord in the coming days, allowing Him to speak to you and bring you the kind of hope that only comes from being connected to God --- the omnipresent and all-powerful King. Cling to Him with tremendous expectation that He will never leave you, and He will always give you the strength and guidance you need to face each day.

Hope from a Savior and King. Allow yourself to be addicted to Him because He gave us life, and He loves us supremely and unconditionally. This is real hope.

Romans 5:2-5, "Through him we have also obtained access by faith into this grace in which we stand, and we rejoice in hope of the glory of God. More than that, we rejoice in our sufferings, knowing that suffering produces endurance, and endurance produces character, and character produces hope, and hope does not put us to shame, because God's love has been poured into our hearts through the Holy Spirit who has been given to us."

Romans 8:24-25, "For in this hope we were saved. Now hope that is seen is not hope. For who hopes for what he sees? But if we hope for what we do not see, we wait for it with patience.

Romans 15:13, "May the God of hope fill you with all joy and peace in believing, so that by the power of the Holy Spirit you may abound in hope."

Charles Nieman, Pastor of Abundant Living Faith Center, El Paso, Texas

Renewal

Renew: according to Webster, it means "to make new or as if new again; to restore." It can also mean "to take up once more; to resume." I renew things all the time --- my driver's license, my auto insurance, contracts for my cell phone and my pest control (both pests, if you ask me). Life seems to be about renewing things that are necessary or desired. Just recently because I have had more time on my hands, I've been going to the library to find great books to devour. When I have to renew those books, it's so easy now with the online system. But renewing my mind is *not* so simple.

I often lose sight of my goals --- the big ones and the little ones. It's easy to commit and then fail, mainly because I made a mental plan but failed to renew my mind. I recently found an eating plan that seemed sensible, practical, and healthy, and I started out strong, but it didn't take long before I began to slip and eat the wrong things again. Why? I failed to renew my mind daily – maybe even hourly – by changing my thinking, not just my plan. I failed because I didn't have a renewal plan in place that took over every time I wanted to eat chocolate cheesecake or steak fries (there should be a diet that includes both of those daily!) But renewal is possible and it will bring success. I just have to be willing to renew my mind first and continually. So how do I do that?

It starts with prayer and scripture. If there is a specific area in which I'm struggling, I seek God's guidance, asking Him to bring to mind a verse that meets my specific need. One scripture God placed on my heart today is, "I can do all things through Christ who strengthens me." I can't just say this once or only write it in my journal. I need to meditate on it all day every day. I need to mutter it repeatedly and mull it over in my mind continually. Then, like any other good habit, it will become a part of my arsenal against failure when Satan tempts me to do the very thing I should not do. It sets my mind for success instead of disaster. It stops me from believing the lies of Satan

. . . lies that tell me I am worthless, that I can't succeed, that God is disappointed in me. Lies. Lies. Lies. But I will slip into that very sense of foreboding that he is trying to create in me if I have not renewed my mind.

I also have to take some other steps for me to be successful. I need to identify my areas and times of extreme weakness and give them to God. I must recognize the places where Satan's darts are most effective and prepare to meditate even more. For example, I am a ball of energy and accomplishment first thing in the morning . . . 5:00 AM to be exact, but at night? I'm a weary, near worthless mess, unable to forge ahead with much of anything. In my eating world, that's very dangerous, especially in my house when everyone is eating popcorn and ice cream in front of the television after 9:00 PM. I have to be prepared ahead of time to avert failure through meditation on scripture and a simple plan to make sure I stay focused on my goal. I have to have healthy choices readily available, and again, I have to ask for God's power through meditating on His Word: "I can do all things through Christ who strengthens me." Even turn down ice cream. And there are bigger issues than ice cream that God can give us the power to defeat.

If I want to know and do the will of God for my life, I must renew my mind continuously. I must immerse myself in God's Word and let the Holy Spirit guide me toward understanding and revelation. In the words of one pastor, if I renew my mind with scripture and prayer, "my lens becomes the truth of God's Word" and then "my life will conform to Jesus Christ until the world around me seems odd." That's what I want: to keep my eyes on Jesus so intently that the worldly issues and behaviors around me don't even make sense. I want to follow Christ, making a difference in the lives of others by doing what God has willed me to do. I want to be tenacious in asking for God's guidance and listening to His voice, whether it whispers quietly or speaks powerfully through the Holy Spirit. I want to obey God radically and allow my destiny to affect the destiny of others. We all have the capability of doing this; we just need to start with renewing our minds.

So today, renew your mind with God's Word. Renew your spirit with His power. Renew your heart with His love. With this plan in place and God's strength and grace on your side, you simply cannot fail.

And as Webster says, you'll be new again.

Romans 12:2, "Do not conform to the pattern of this world, but be transformed by the renewing of your mind. Then you will be able to test and approve what God's will is--his good, pleasing and perfect will."

Messy Blessings

Blessings can be messy. Yesterday we had four of our children, two sons-in-law, and three of our grandchildren at our home. We started the day with coffee and breakfast, and then the plans began. A trip to the farm --- swimming, fishing, swinging, picking blackberries --- it was wonderful and tiring, and then we made our way back to our house. Lunch, swimming, watering flowers, and dinner, and while the adults cooked, the children played. They played in every single room that had anything that even hinted at being a toy. They found new uses for decorations I brought home from school. They colored and painted and worked on puzzles and built with blocks. They played drums, played our two pianos, and ran room to room, almost giddy with excitement at being together in a house filled with so much to do. And then? Harper found a squash from our garden, turning it into her personal phone. "Hewwo," she said as she carried her squash phone from room to room, and then it was on. They all got vegetables and had a rich conversation phone to phone. . . it was both wonderful and hysterically funny to watch.

It was messy!

This morning I woke up and headed to my "office" to have some quiet time, and I could hardly find a place to walk that wasn't covered in puzzle pieces and toys. I quietly and happily sat down on the floor to put everything away, and I thought about the incredible blessings of having my family close at hand. Is that blessing messy? You better believe it. But is it worth it? Oh, yes, it is worth having to pick up toys and wipe counters every single day.

And the lesson: God's blessings often come in messy packages that require us to do some work.

God has promised in scripture that He will guide us and order the steps of our lives. He has promised to give us a hope and a future.

But in those promises, some of the most incredible blessings come with some mess. Example? I have visited Salkehatchie work sites this week, watching the young people put roofs on houses that desperately needed repair. The workers there are being blessed beyond measure, and the recipients of the work are the same. But in the yards, there was sawdust, saws, ladders, old shingles, coolers full of water . . . a mess. Eventually the mess will be cleaned and cleared away, and both workers and home owners will have been touched by the hand of God through the service of people who, because of their love for Him, also love His people. The mess is worth it; we just have to see beyond the mess and know that God is at work.

Another example: I love to speak and sing about God, anytime and anywhere I am invited. When I am given a topic on which to speak, the beginning of my planning is messy. I pray, asking for God's guidance to make sure I am in line with what He wants me to say. As He begins to move in my heart through the Holy Spirit, I begin to scribble ideas in my journal. When I am very clear about the direction of the talk, I begin to write a rough draft, but before I finish, I have revised and revised and revised . . . making very sure that what I am saying is in line with God, His desires, and His truth. My original copy of the talk and song choices are messy with ink and scribbles and changes, but at the end of the plan, I am blessed, and God always --- **ALWAYS** --- uses those talks to bless the listeners based on His plan. He never fails to make that happen. It starts out as a mess but ends up as a blessing.

If you ask God to make His desires your desires, He will do it. But you cannot live afraid of where His plans might take you or how messy it might require your life to be. If it is His plan, He will provide for you, giving you the strength to deal with the messes and come out on the other side, blessed beyond measure for giving your life over to His service.

I encourage you to ask Him today for His plans for your life and then trust Him to take care of the details. You will be blessed beyond measure, and the messes? They won't even matter in the big picture because your eyes will be on God, and when you are looking at Him, you really can't see anything else.

Messy and blessed . . . Amen.

Numbers 6:24-26, "The Lord bless you and keep you;
the Lord make his face shine on you and be gracious to you;
the Lord turn his face toward you and give you peace."

Epilogue -- Come Home

There's a wonderful children's book I love called *Cat, You Better Come Home.* It's the strange story of a beloved cat who leaves home in a huff and heads to greener pastures. He makes wealthy friends and finds himself living the high life, but throughout the story, the cat's owner keeps repeating these words:

"O CAT, YOU BETTER COME HOME. You're a top cat now and you're riding high but they'll dump you in the river when the well runs dry, so CAT, YOU BETTER COME HOME."

The story is funny, and the made-up words and the rhyming patterns make it a joy to read aloud, but recently it has made me think about how often we go away from "home," looking for greener pastures. And when we do, throughout our story, God is constantly saying, "My Child, you better come home." I think it's time to listen.

God's voice has been calling out to us longer than we even realize. He calls out to us through the beauty and majesty of His creations. He calls out to us through the circumstances of our lives. He calls out to us through the emptiness in our hearts, asking us to come home to Him, our only true Father. His prevenient grace --- grace that "comes before" --- has been drawing us to him all our lives. Many have answered that call and been made whole by his justifying grace --- the grace that redeems us. But here's the problem, especially for believers.

It's so easy to get complacent about our home with God. We can slip into apathy or a take-for-granted attitude, and we go about living our lives, seeking the luxuries and accolades that the world offers. We begin to think somehow that we can do it without Him . . . without His Hand, without His minute-by-minute guidance, and without His grace.

Well, we can't. And yet, just like the prodigal son, we slip away from the one relationship that trumps all others.

But here's the good news: God, just like the cat's owner, is constantly calling us to come home. Just like the father in the story of the prodigal son, he is waiting to welcome us with open arms and throw a party when we choose to run to Him. In the cat story, when he finally goes home, he finds a warm bed beside a cool breeze, a place to rest and heal from his extravagant lifestyle, and the peace found in safety. We can have that, too. When we come home to God, the Father, He is there with His promise to pull us out of the miry clay and set our feet upon a solid rock. He is there to cover us with His wings of protection. He is there to love us with a passion that is like no other. Why would we look anywhere else to be fulfilled?

At the end of the story, when the cat comes home, his owner says this:

"Oh CAT, I'M GLAD YOU CAME HOME! No need to explain, my old cat friend, I'm just glad to have you back again. YES, CAT, I'M SO GLAD YOU CAME HOME!"

And with God, there is no need to explain, but instead, we need to ask forgiveness for running away, and fall into His arms of love and acceptance. We need to be eternally grateful for a Father who calls to us and then welcomes us home into His awesome presence. And then? We need to learn from our past, live with a grateful heart and a servant's spirit today, and appreciate the future God has in store for us when we let His dreams become our dreams.

When we do this, I know that God will say, "Oh, Child of mine, I'm so glad you came home!" And in the words of Travis Cottrell's version of "Just As I Am," we will be "welcomed with open arms, praise God, just as I am." Run home today . . . just as you are . . . and be welcomed into the arms of God, your heavenly Father.

Proverbs 18:10, "The name of the LORD is a fortified tower; the righteous run to it and are safe."

Thanks to my precious sister, Bobbie, a lover of books, who shared this incredible story with my children in 1995! This devotional is dedicated to you!

Works Cited

Keillor, Garrison. Cat, You Better Come Home. Viking Children's Books, 1995. Print.

London, Jack. The Call of the Wild. St. Paul: EMC/Paradigm Publishing, 1998. Print.

Lucado, Max. The Lucado Inspirational Reader. Thomas Nelson Publishers, 2011. Print.

Tiegreen, Chris. The One Year At His Feet Devotional. Carol Stream: Tyndale House Publishers, 2003. Print.

Warren, Rick, Daniel Amen, and Mark Hyman. The Daniel Plan. Zondervan Press. 2013. Print.

CPSIA information can be obtained
at www.ICGtesting.com
Printed in the USA
FFOW05n2344010315